TROUT

© Alissa Crandall

TROUT
An Angler's Guide

TIMOTHY FREW

MALLARD PRESS

MALLARD PRESS
An imprint of BDD Promotional Book Company, Inc.
666 Fifth Avenue
New York, New York 10103

A FRIEDMAN GROUP BOOK

Published by MALLARD PRESS
An imprint of BDD Promotional Book Company, Inc.
666 Fifth Avenue
New York, New York 10103

Mallard Press and its accompanying design and logo are trademarks of BDD Promotional Book Company, Inc.

Copyright © 1991 by Michael Friedman Publishing Group, Inc.

First published in the United States of America in 1991 by The Mallard Press.

All rights reserved. No part of this publication may be reproduced, stored in a retrieval system or transmitted, in any form or by any means, electronic, mechanical, photocopying, recording, or otherwise, without the prior written permission of the publisher.

ISBN 0-792-45294-1

TROUT: An Angler's Guide
was prepared and produced by
Michael Friedman Publishing Group, Inc.
15 West 26th Street
New York, New York 10010

Editor: Sharon Kalman
Art Director: Jeff Batzli
Designer: Susan Livingston
Photo Researcher: Daniella Jo Nilva

Typeset by EAC/Interface
Color separations by Universal Colour Scanning Ltd.
Printed and bound in Hong Kong by Leefung-Asco Printers Ltd.

Dedication
To my father, William Frew, who caught the first trout I ever tasted.

Acknowledgments
I would like to acknowledge my editor, Sharon Kalman, for making sure I finished the book; the designer, Sue Livingston, for making the book beautiful and for sifting through countless fish photos in search of just the right picture; and to Herbert Shaffner, a fishing friend who was always at the ready with suggestions and valuable input.

TABLE OF CONTENTS

© Erwin & Peggy Bauer

INTRODUCTION

8

CHAPTER ONE

The Trout Angler's Arsenal

12

CHAPTER TWO

The Brook Trout

30

CHAPTER THREE

Rainbow Trout

46

CHAPTER FOUR

Steelhead

62

CHAPTER FIVE

Brown Trout

80

CHAPTER SIX

Cutthroat

94

CHAPTER SEVEN

The Lake Trout

108

BIBLIOGRAPHY &
RECOMMENDED READING

124

INDEX

126

© Wally Eberhart

INTRODUCTION

The trout is probably the most studied, the most written about, and the most sought after freshwater gamefish in the world. Through the years there have been thousands of books, pamphlets, magazines,

Trout

INTRODUCTION

Few experiences in sport are as enjoyable as pulling a tenacious trout from a cool mountain stream. Most expert anglers believe that fly fishing is the most challenging method for catching trout.

video tapes, television shows, and even academic papers dedicated to the subject of trout fishing. Much of this material focuses on techniques for catching trout; some simply center on the behavior and characteristics of the trout itself. Many of the world's finest pieces of outdoor writing have been dedicated to the subject of trout and trout fishing. *The Compleat Angler* by Isaac Walton, *Trout* by Ray Bergman, *The Year of the Trout* by Steve Raymond, *Trout Bum* by John Geirach, and *A River Runs Through It* by Norman Maclean are just a few of the many fine titles that transcend outdoors writing and enter into the realm of literature.

Why has a fish as small and seemingly insignificant as the trout been the subject of so much creative effort? Why do anglers, year after year, devote so much time, energy, and money toward catching just a few of these fish? Why has the trout become a virtual mythological symbol for today's outdoorsman? Perhaps the answers to these questions can only be fully understood by those people who have experienced the challenge of battling a tenacious brown in a cool mountain stream. Only when you experience trout fishing firsthand can you appreciate its allure.

Whether you are fishing for steelhead on the Umpqua, browns on the Beaverkill, lakers on the Athabasca, cutthroats on the Nimpkish, or rainbows in your neighborhood creek, it is important to understand the behavior, habitat, and feeding characteristics of your quarry. Each type of trout behaves by its own set of rules, which are determined both by genetic makeup and the peculiarities of its aquatic environment. The more you know about the trout and its world, the better your chances will be for catching them. This book offers guidelines for locating and catching the most commonly fished for trout species in North America. Each chapter looks at the habitat, range, spawning habits, feeding characteristics, migratory trends, and appearance of a particular trout species, as well as provides pointers on equipment and angling techniques.

Any advice, however, should be looked at with a degree of skepticism. Even if you read all of the books by the world's greatest anglers and follow their advice to a tee, you still may not have fishing success. In fact, you will most likely find that many "fishing experts" contradict each other on many very basic points. Such is the nature of fishing that no two anglers will agree on the proper way to catch the same fish on the same river. All of the suggestions put forth in this book should be taken as just that—suggestions, things to try out when you're on the stream or lake. Only by actually fishing will you become a good angler. Besides, casting your fly to a hungry trout is much more enjoyable than merely reading about it.

Chapter 1

The Trout Angler's Arsenal

The trout is by nature a very sedentary and skittish fish. The angler must learn to bring the fly, lure, or bait directly to the fish while creating a minimum of disturbance. Trout are very intelligent and are not easily

Once its simple techniques are mastered, fly fishing can be the most rewarding of all styles of fishing. At right, an angler takes in the scenic beauty while fishing for trout on the Snake River in Idaho.

fooled by even the most clever angler. If a fly or lure looks at all suspicious or acts in an unnatural way, these wary fish will pay no attention to it. Trout fishing can be accurately described as a battle of wits between angler and fish, played out in the underwater environment of a small river, stream, or lake. With all the different types, weights, and sizes of fishing outfits and all the different lures, spoons, spinners, flies, and baits in the angler's arsenal, it sometimes seems amazing that the small freshwater *piscis* known as the trout even has a chance. Yet, time and time again, the trout will beguile even the most seasoned of anglers. Such is the sport of trout fishing.

Trout can be found in a wide variety of aquatic environments, from wide, fast-flowing rivers to deep lakes, to small mountain streams. Precision delivery and natural presentation are a must for any type of success in trout angling. Because of this, it is important that anglers have fishing outfits that are well suited to the type of fishing they are doing. Fresh-water fishing equipment can be divided into three distinct categories: fly fishing, spinning, and bait casting. Each outfit has its own individual nuances, and its own advantages and disadvantages. This chapter serves as a general overview of the different types of fishing outfits available to the trout angler. It is designed to help beginning anglers examine their fishing needs and to choose the best type of outfit to fit their situation. If you wish to delve further into the seemingly never-ending world of fishing tackle, you might read a few of the many books dedicated solely to that subject. (See Bibliography and Recommended Readings for a few suggestions.)

FLY FISHING

One of the most beautiful sights in all of fishing—not counting, of course, a large steelhead breaching at the end of your line—is the graceful, delicate, and accurate cast of an expert fly angler. The line arches gently through the air as the angler casts to and fro, gaining momentum. Finally, one last long backswing. Just as the line plays out completely behind the angler, he or she whips it forward into a perfect, rolling, arching cast.

It is the simple, elegant motion of the fly cast that attracts the majority of anglers to fly fishing. On the other hand, many experienced bait casters are intimidated by the complexity of catching trout on a fly and never even attempt it. This is a shame; for despite the mystique surrounding the sport, fly fishing is really based on just a few simple techniques and concepts. Once these basics are learned, the angler can go forth and enthusiastically pursue this sport, always striving to improve. And that is perhaps the most enjoyable aspect of fly fishing; your technique can

… The Trout Angler's Arsenal

Trout

High-quality equipment is important to the success of any fishing expedition—whether you are on your local trout stream or on the Flathead River in Montana (left). Modern graphite rods (near right) provide a good combination of strength and elasticity and are quickly becoming the rods of choice among most anglers, while bamboo rods (far right) are still favorites among many traditionalists.

always be improved upon, but it can never be completely perfected.

Because the casting and proper presentation of the fly is so important in this type of fishing, proper equipment is crucial to any type of success. The next few pages serve as a primer to the different components that make up a fly-fishing outfit. If you are a newcomer who is just becoming interested in fly fishing, I would heartily recommend you read a few of the many excellent beginner's books about fly fishing. *Fly Fishing: A Beginner's Guide* by David Lee and *Trout on a Fly* by Lee Wulff are two good places to start.

Rods

The rod is arguably the single most important piece of equipment in the fly angler's repertoire. It is through the action of this device that the angler delivers the fly to its destination. If you have a poor-quality rod, or one that is not suited to your particular angling situation, you will most likely not be able to cast accurately—and if you can't take the fly to the fish, you can't catch the fish.

The Trout Angler's Arsenal

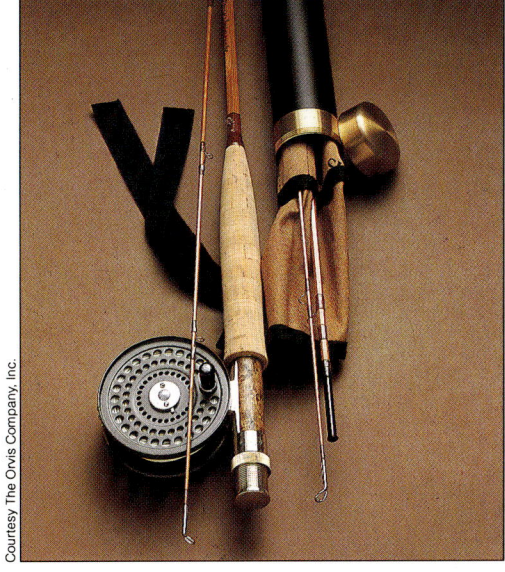

Fly fishing differs from both spin casting and bait casting in that you actually cast the line, which pulls the fly along with it, instead of casting the lure or bait. The weight of the line bends, or loads, the fly rod on the backcast, then as you bring the rod forward, the rod springs back and helps to propel the fly to its destination.

Rod Materials

The composition of the fly rod has changed drastically over the past 150 years. Originally all rods were made of wood...that is until craftsmen discovered the benefits of bamboo cane at the end of the eighteenth century. Soon nearly all fly rods were made from this resilient material. Over the past century, modern technology has provided the fly angler with a variety of choices when buying a rod. Of course the bamboo rod is still manufactured, but now it is joined by rods made of fiberglass and graphite, as well.

- **Bamboo** fly rods are the most carefully constructed and responsive artifacts available to the fly angler. Even though some graphite and fiberglass rods have equaled, or even surpassed, the bamboo in overall performance, none can come even close to matching its grace, beauty, and as many fly traditionalists claim, its "feel." Because of the high level of craftsmanship involved in their construction, bamboo rods are very expensive. They can range in price from six hundred to several thousand dollars. While this price tag may seem prohibitive to most anglers, it can be looked upon as an investment, for these rods continue to perform well year after year and even generation after generation.

- **Fiberglass** was the first material to pose a challenge to the bamboo rod industry. When fiberglass rods came on the scene after the 1940s, they were the lightest, strongest, most affordable rods available. Today, however, the bamboo rod is still going strong, and it is the fiberglass rod that is most threatened by the development of graphite. While it is relatively lightweight, fiberglass is still heavier than graphite, and graphite rods offer more power and higher sensitivity for a comparable price.

- **Graphite** is a product of the carbon-fiber technology developed by the modern aerospace industry. It is a resilient, lightweight fiber that has a "high modulus of elasticity," which means that it provides more snap for the fly angler. Since graphite rods were first introduced in the early 1970s, they have taken the fishing industry by storm. They combine light weight, high power, and a good "feel" in a rod that performs well in virtually any fishing situation. While high-quality graphite rods are generally more expensive than glass rods, their added performance and versatility more than makes up for the price difference.

Rod Length

The length of your fly rod will depend on a number of different factors: the size and type of fish you are catching, the size of the river you're fishing, and your own personal preference. If you are fishing for large, hard-fighting fish, you may want to use heavier line, which in turn requires a longer rod. If you are fishing for small browns or brookies in shallow, clear streams, you may want to use a shorter rod for more accurate casts.

For most trout-fishing situations, a fly rod between 7 and 9 feet (2 to 3 m) loaded with a medium-weight line will suffice. A 9- or 10-foot (3-m) rod loaded with heavy line may be necessary when fishing for steelhead or salmon on wide, fast-flowing rivers, but many a battling fish has been caught using much lighter equipment. Perhaps the best and most versatile outfit for a beginning fly angler is an 8½-foot (3-m) rod, loaded with 5- or 6-weight line.

Line Weight

The weight of your line will depend largely on the type of situations in which you will be fishing. The chart found on page 19 serves as a rough guide to help you match your line weight to your particular fishing situation. The weight numbers,

The Trout Angler's Arsenal

Line Weights

Line Weight	Fishing Situation
2 to 4	The lightest fly lines available, these weights are for the experienced fly angler who is fishing for small, easily frightened browns and brookies in narrow, clear streams. They create a minimum of disturbance, but are difficult to cast.
4 to 6	The best line weight for a variety of trout-fishing situations. Good for casting virtually any type of fly, from small dry flies and nymphs to long hairy streamers and bucktails.
6 to 8	These heavy lines are designed for catching big fish in wide, powerful rivers and deep lakes, any situation where long, powerful casts are required. Good for steelhead and big lake cutthroats or browns.
8 to 10	These heavier lines require a stiff fly rod for effective casting. The heavyweight line is used primarily for saltwater fly fishing or for big steelhead and salmon.

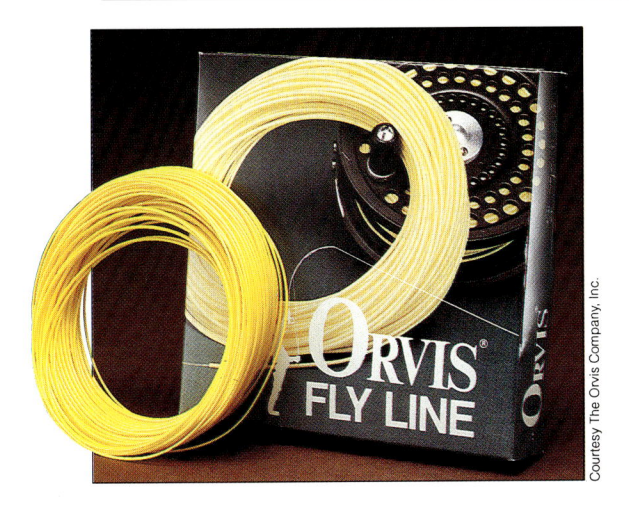

which go from one to twelve, were developed by the American Fishing Tackle Manufacturers Association (AFTMA). They correspond to the weight in grains of the first 30 feet (10 m) of line. For example, a 5-weight line weighs 140 grains and a 10-weight line weighs 280 grains. The actual weight in grains is not important, but the corresponding AFTMA number is.

Line Taper

The taper of a fly line—the gradual decrease in thickness—helps control both the accuracy and distance of the cast. There are several different configurations to choose from, each with its own set of casting characteristics.

The most basic and inexpensive type of fly line is the *level line*. This line has the same diameter from one end to the other. As a result, it does not provide the angler with very good casting distance or accuracy. The level line is largely outmoded and only used by a handful of anglers.

The *double-taper line* is essentially two fly lines in one. It has the same fine taper at each end of the line, which means once one end becomes worn, the angler can simply reverse the line and use the other end. The tapered end makes for smooth, accurate casting and a soft presentation of the line. The double taper is the most popular and expensive of all fly lines.

Over recent years, the *weight forward line* has become increasingly popular among anglers who need extra distance in their casts. Most of the weight of this fly line is concentrated up front, in the first 30 feet (10 m) of line, tapering off to a thinner diameter at the middle and back sections. These lines do allow the angler to cast long and hard, but at the expense of some accuracy and delicacy of presentation.

For anglers who require even longer casts, such as those fishing for western steelhead, the *shooting taper*, or *shooting head* line may be the configuration of choice. Similar to the weight-forward taper, the shooting taper has a weighted front section; however, the taper is then attached to a small diameter running line instead of the traditional running line. Since virtually all of the weight on this line is up front, the angler can unhurl some amazingly long, quick casts.

Line Density

The gravity of the fly line refers to whether or not the line sinks, floats, or does both. Most beginning fly-fishing books recommend that the novice use *floating line*. This is the basic line for fly fishing. While its primary use is for shallow, wet flies and a few dry flies, it can also be successfully used for fishing streamers and nymphs in moderately swift and deep water. Because the line floats on the top of the water, it allows the angler to see the fish strike his/her fly.

The oldest type of fly line is the *sinking line*. As its name states, this line sinks from one end to the other. Today, the angler has a wide selection of choices as to how fast or deep a sinking line will sink. In general, these lines are used for fishing deep lakes or extremely strong, deep rivers where the fish are feeding on the bottom.

The *intermediate line* attempts to combine the best of both worlds. It is an extremely versatile line that uniformly sinks just a few inches below the surface. The disadvantage of this line is that it is difficult to cast due to its harder finish, and you can't see the fish strike because the line is underwater.

One step up from the intermediate line is the *floating-sinking line*, or *sink-tip line*. This is essentially a floating fly line with a sinking tip. This allows the angler to fish below the surface, with the added advantage of seeing the line. Floating-sinking lines come in a variety of configurations: 10-foot (3-m) sinking tips, 20-foot (6-m) sinking tips, and 30-foot (9-m) sinking tips.

REELS

The fly reel is probably the least important piece of equipment in the fly angler's arsenal. Its primary function is to store line. It is never used for casting and is only very seldom used to help haul the fish in. The fly angler instead uses the hands to strip line in and out when casting or playing a fish. That is not to say, however, that you should cut corners and buy a cheap reel when purchasing a fly outfit. Poorly made reels always break—an extremely frustrating experience when you've just hooked a hard-fighting fish that is making a desperate run for freedom.

There are several factors to keep in mind when looking for the correct fly reel for your outfit. The first is *reel capacity*, the amount of fly line and backing line—the braided line wound on the reel and tied to the fly line—that the reel can hold. A quality reel will hold between 50 and 75 yards (45 and 67 m) of backing line in addition to the proper amount of fly line. The actual amount of fly line a reel will hold depends on the weight of the line. When fishing for small trout, such as brooks or browns, the angler should have a reel that can hold between 75 and 100 yards (67 and 90 m) of 4-weight line. When fishing for larger and stronger fish, such as steelhead trout, the angler may need a slightly larger reel that is capable of holding between 150 and

Even though the fly reel is perhaps the fly angler's least important piece of equipment, it still pays to buy a high-quality reel. Orvis, a highly respected name in the fly-fishing industry, makes quality reels for just about every pocketbook.

160 yards (135 and 144 m) of 8-weight line. Saltwater fly-anglers and anglers going after extremely large Atlantic salmon should have reels that are large enough to hold about 300 to 350 yards (270 to 315 m) of 9- to 11-weight line.

Weight is another important consideration when purchasing a fly reel. The weight of your reel should be matched to the weight of your rod so that the entire outfit is properly balanced. A poorly balanced outfit will make accurate casting very difficult. Quality trout-fishing rods weigh between 2½ and 6 ounces (70 and 168 g), while steelhead, salmon, and saltwater rods generally weigh between 9 and 12 ounces (252 and 336 g). The weight of the reel depends on the size and weight of the rod.

The *drag system* is the mechanical device that puts friction on the reel as a fish is pulling off line. Most fly reels have a knob-adjusted drag system, which uses triangular-shaped pawls to create friction. As the angler turns the knob the spring-loaded drag system will put more pressure on the pawls, thereby creating more drag on the line. A quality reel will have two or three pawls, which make them reliable and easy to adjust, while most cheaper reels only have one pawl, making it a little more difficult for you.

There are hundreds of different types of flies available to the average angler. Many times, choosing the right fly for a particular situation results from a combination of science, myth, and trial and error.

FLIES

There are hundreds upon hundreds of fly patterns readily available to the angler. Sporting such unusual names as Ratfaced MacDougal, Pale Evening Dun, Black Bomber, and Wooley Worm, the vast array of these colorful, feathery flies can easily boggle the mind of the angler making his/her first venture into the world of fly fishing. Basically, flies are divided into two main categories: specifics, which attempt to match as closely as possible particular insects, and attractors, which imitate no particular insect, but instead are designed to attract the trout's attention through a combination of movement and color.

Flies are also divided into different subcategories pertaining to what they are imitating or suggesting, and to how they are fished. Dry flies are designed to closely imitate hatching aquatic insects and are fished on the surface. Wet flies imitate or suggest a variety of subaquatic insects or minnows and are usually fished just below the surface. Streamers, or bucktails, imitate minnows or small fish. Terrestrials suggest land insects that fall or are blown into the water, such as grasshoppers or ants. And finally, nymphs imitate the larval forms of aquatic insects.

There is no surefire method for determining exactly which fly to use on what stream in a certain situation. The seemingly simple act of choosing a fly has now become a veritable art form. The best advice is to start with a wide variety of proven fly patterns and sizes, ask the advice of anglers who are familiar with a particular stream, and, finally, experiment. Throughout this book are suggestions on which fly patterns to use for certain types of fish. The flies mentioned here are all fairly well known patterns used by thousands of anglers across North America. That does not mean, however, that they will always work. Nor does it mean that another type of fly not mentioned here will not be better. For more information on flies and the art of choosing them, I suggest you pick up a few of the many books on the subject. One of the best is *Selective Trout* by Doug Swisher and Carl Richards.

The Trout Angler's Arsenal

Spin-casting and spinning reels are the easiest of all reels to operate. Their fixed spool system eliminates the backlashes and bird's nests that sometimes occur with bait-casting reels.

SPINNING TACKLE

After its introduction in the 1940s, the spinning reel quickly revolutionized North American fishing tackle. This fixed-spool system made casting even the lightest of lures a breeze. No longer would the angler be plagued by the debilitating "backlashes" and "bird's nests" that occurred all too often with the bait-casting reel.

In a spinning outfit, the reel itself remains stationary and the line rolls off the reel in loops. The guides in a spinning rod are set up so that they are wide at the butt end of the rod and gradually get smaller toward the tip. The large guides gather the loops as they come off the reel, then as the guides get smaller, so do the loops. This helps reduce friction and increase casting distance.

Spinning reels come in two styles: open-faced and closed-faced. The closed-faced reel—otherwise known as a spin-casting reel, as opposed to a spinning reel—has a cone-shaped housing that covers the spool. The cast is controlled by a button on the back of the reel. You simply hold the button down to grab the line before you cast and then release it as you whip the rod forward. While these simple spin-casting reels are easy to operate, they do not give you the control of the open-faced reel and they cut down on casting distance due to friction caused by the reel housing.

Open-faced reels have no housing and offer more control than spin-casting reels. A bail holds the line in place when not casting. In order to cast, push the bail back and drape the loose line over your index finger.

Lift your finger off the line as you cast. This reel gives you added control because you can add varying amounts of friction to the line for pinpoint accuracy.

It is important not to skimp on quality when buying a spinning reel. Cheap reels will almost always break or tangle your line at the most inopportune moments. It is also impor-

Ultralight spinning outfits can provide some very exciting fishing, where casting accuracy is a must.

tant to get a spinning reel that fits into the reel seat tightly and is properly balanced to your rod. If you are buying a new reel for an old rod, always bring in your rod to make sure your new purchase fits properly.

Freshwater spinning outfits are divided into four groups: ultralight, light, medium, and heavy. Ultralight spinning rods run between 4½ and 6 feet (137 to 183 cm) in length. They are extremely whippy and can cast lures that weigh as little as 1/16 of an ounce. Because ultralights are so light and short, their casting range is limited, making them a poor choice for fishing large bodies of water. They do, however, make for great sport for the experienced angler who is fishing for skittish trout in small, clear streams. In the right hands, ultralights are deadly accurate. They can be used for casting between jagged, line snagging structures, underneath low hanging bushes, and for placing a lure right in front of a wary old brown. These 1½ to 2 ounce (42 to 56 g) rods cast thin, wispy lines and small lures; therefore, high quality is of the utmost importance. A top-of-the-line, ultralight spinning reel with a delicate drag setting is required to avoid an afternoon of frustrations. These outfits use lines of 3-pound (1-kg) test or lower, so taking even a small, half-pound fish can be quite a challenge. If you are a novice who is looking for a good everyday rod, the ultralight is a poor choice. Leave these feathery outfits to the experts.

The lightweight spinning outfit is a much more practical choice for fishing freshwater streams, rivers, and lakes. This outfit offers a bit more versatility for the angler going after a variety of fish under 2 or 3 pounds (.9 or 1 kg). Ranging in length from 5½ to 7 feet (165 to 210 cm), lightweight rods can be matched with most freshwater reels; however, lighter reels will give you a

TROUT

The Trout Angler's Arsenal

Three determined anglers take in some early spring fishing in Roaring River State Park, Missouri.

more balanced outfit. These rods will cast monofilament lines from 4- to 6-pound (2- to 3-kg) test and lures weighing between 1/8 and 3/8 of an ounce. This makes them ideal for most trout fishing situations. They can cast relatively far with a good degree of accuracy, so unless you are consistently going after steelhead or salmon, lightweight is the best everyday fishing choice.

Medium-weight spinning outfits also feature 5½- to 7-foot (165- to 210-cm) rods, but with stiffer butt ends, less taper, and more backbone for handling larger, stronger fish. These rods can accommodate most spinning reels that are filled with 6- to 8-pound (3- to 4-kg) test and will cast lures from 3/8 to 1 ounce with distance and accuracy. This is the spinning outfit of choice for the serious trout angler. It is heavy enough for hauling in ferocious steelhead and even for trolling larger lakers, yet it can also handle line light enough for catching wary browns and brookies.

Heavyweight spinning outfits range from 6 to 9 feet (2 to 3 m) and are used solely for the largest and strongest freshwater fish such as steelhead, salmon, lake trout, muskies, big carp, and pike. These long, stiff rods can only be matched up with large spinning reels and strong line—between 8- and 25-pound (4- and 11-kg) test. They will handle lures and sinkers weighing 1/2 to two ounces (14 to 56 g), limiting them to only the largest of fish. Because of their lack of versatility, heavyweights are not good outfits for the everyday trout angler. Their trout applications are pretty much limited to casting long for steelhead and deep trolling for lake trout, so most anglers are better off spending their money on a high-quality lightweight or medium-weight rod.

BAIT-CASTING TACKLE

Following the advent of spinning tackle after World War II, it seemed as if the days of the back-lashing, knuckle-scraping bait casters were over. In a sense, they were. Many anglers immediately put their old bait casters in the closet in favor of the new, easy-to-use spinning outfits.

Over the past twenty-five years, however, bait-casting technology has been improved upon to such an extent that, once again, many serious anglers are making the bait caster their outfit of choice.

When the reels were cast, the spool, gears, and handle all revolved simultaneously making it difficult for the angler to control. If he/she did not apply thumb pressure at just the right time to drop the lure in the water, a serious backlash would occur, causing the line to tangle up in what became known as a bird's nest. In addition, when a big fish was on the line of an old bait caster, the spool and handle would both start spinning furiously, often jamming the angler's thumb or scraping his/her knuckles.

Most of today's quality bait casters are built with magnetic anti-backlash technology and level-wind mechanisms (a guide that evenly places retrieved line on the spool). The most significant development in bait-casting equipment is free-spool casting. This means that only the spool rotates during the cast, making it much easier to control the flow of the line and to avoid backlash.

Bait-casting outfits are divided into three categories: lightweights, medium-weights, and heavyweights. Lightweight rods run from 5 to 6½ feet (150 to 195 cm) in length and have a very limber action. These outfits, which can cast light lures and baits weighing between 1/4 and 1/2 ounce, are designed primarily for crappie fishing and have very few applications for the trout angler.

Medium weight rods are actually a bit shorter than lightweights (between 4½ and 6 feet [1 and 2 m]), however, they are much stiffer, have reinforced butts, less taper, and can cast slightly bigger lures and baits (between 3/8 and 3/4 of an ounce). These outfits are designed to be worked in small, overgrown creeks and rivers where accurate casting is a must. This makes them a good choice for a variety of fish including many big trout.

Heavyweight bait-casting rods are about the same length as lightweight

Manufacturers have made great strides in eliminating the debilitating backlash that was so prevalent with the bait-casting reels of yesteryear. Even so, many anglers prefer the simplicity of spinning equipment for most angling situations.

rods, but much stiffer and more powerful. These stable rods can easily handle lures and baits as heavy as 1½ to 2 ounces (42 to 56 g) and can throw line testing between 15 to 20 pounds (7 to 9 kg). Most freshwater angling, however, does not require line any heavier than 15-pound (7-kg) test. These are popular outfits for snagging big black bass, pike, and muskies. For the trout angler, however, heavyweight bait-casting rods are only applicable to catching steelhead and trolling for big lake trout.

Even with all of the improvements over the past twenty-five years, the bait caster is still a fairly tricky outfit to handle. While backlash has been cut down, it has not been totally eliminated. It takes a lot of practice and good timing to effectively cast with this outfit. In the right hands, the bait caster can be a deadly accurate tool. It is a very popular outfit among bass anglers who require precise casting, yet enough backbone to pull lunkers out of a heavy structure. The trout angler, however, may be better served with a good quality spinning or fly outfit.

Chapter 2

THE BROOK TROUT

When the first white settlers came to North America, they were dependent on their old European tradition of trout fishing for both survival and recreation. At the time, there was only one type of trout living in the

Natural populations of brook trout were once plentiful across North America. Today, however, most brookies caught are stockers from hatcheries such as this one in Wyoming (right).

cool, swift waters of the northeast—the brook trout. The Native Americans had been fishing for brookies for hundreds of years using nets, fishing spears, and bows and arrows. They must have thought the displaced Europeans strange with their curious-looking long rods and hooked lines.

During the early days of European settlement in North America, the brook trout was abundant in almost every river, stream, brook, lake, and pond from Labrador, west to Saskatchewan, and south through the Alleghenies to northern Georgia. Brookies provided good sport and ample food and remained the most popular North American game fish for over one hundred years. Eventually the brook trout was introduced in the West, from California to Alaska and then later in the Rocky Mountain states.

Today, the brook trout remains a very popular fish in areas where it is still plentiful. Unfortunately, the steady encroachment of civilization has taken quite a toll on the brookie. The growth of cities, with their huge

The Brook Trout

populations and industrial backbones, and the clearing of wooded lands for farming and lumber have made many of the brook trout's natural waters virtually uninhabitable for the sensitive fish. The environmental problems of acid rain and siltation, which currently threaten all types of North American game fish, have had a particularly adverse effect on the brook trout. These fish require very cool, pristine waters to survive. Even slight increases in water temperature and relatively low levels of industrial pollution can lead to the fish's demise.

Fish hatchery services breed millions of brook trout every year for stocking programs across North America. The brook trout, however, is a very cooperative fish for the angler. If not startled, it will strike most baits, lures, or flies that are presented in a natural way. Unfortunately, because of this relative ease of catch and the brookie's popularity, the vast majority of stocked brook trout end up in the angler's game box and do not survive to form natural populations.

Despite its common name, the brook trout is not really a trout at all. Its scientific name is *Salvelinus fontinalis*, which classifies it as a salmonid and a member of the char group, like the Dolly Varden or the lake trout. To most anglers, however, the brook trout is considered a trout through and through, which is why it is included in this volume. Other common names for *Salvelinus fontinalis* are: speckled trout, native trout, eastern brook trout, mountain trout, red trout, squaretails, and brookies.

The brook trout is one of the most colorful of all freshwater fish, especially during the fall spawning season. Its back is blue-green with a slight red or yellowish tint. It also has wavy, wormlike markings on its back and sides down to the lateral line, as well as red spots within blue halos on its sides. The belly of the brook trout is ordinarily white; however, it can take on a reddish tint in older males. Its relatively large pectoral, pelvic, and anal fins can range in color from orange to red, and its dorsal fin is usually dark, with lighter undulating lines.

The Brook Trout

The brook trout is one of the most colorful game fish in North America. Its most distinguishing markings are red dots surrounded by blue halos running along either side.

While most brookies remain in fresh water for their entire lives, some of those located near coastal areas will venture into marine waters. When living in salt water, the brook trout's coloring and markings fade. Their backs turn bluish green, their sides turn silvery, and their bellies turn pure white, much like the steelhead trout. Once the fish return to fresh water, however, they regain their colorful appearance.

Most brook trout caught today are relatively small, rarely growing to more than 10 to 12 inches (25 to 30 cm) and weighing a pound or two (up to three-quarters of a kilogram). Large natural brook trout, from 5 to 8 pounds (2 to 3 kg), can still be caught in large rivers and lakes of the wilderness areas of eastern Canada, the Rocky Mountain states, Maine, and Vermont, as well as in Argentina and Chile, where the fish was introduced. As a general rule in North America, the farther south you go, the smaller the fish will be. The largest brook trout, 14½ pounds (5 kg), 21 inches (53 cm), was caught in 1916 on the Nipigon River, Ontario, Canada.

Trout

Brookies love small, shallow, cool streams. It is best to look for them in moderate currents, around boulders, submerged logs, small dams, and other structures.

Part of the brook trout's immense popularity over the years is due to the fact that it is relatively easy to catch. Brook trout, especially "stockers," will go for a wide variety of baits, lures, spinners, and flies. Brookies are not picky eaters. They will strike hard and fast, and once hooked will put up a powerful and determined fight. They will dart across and down stream, trying to foul your line on a submerged log or rock. Unlike other types of trout, brookies almost never jump. They will stay underwater and fight until they either snag your line and escape, or roll over from exhaustion.

The larger the brook trout, the harder it is to hook, and the more skillful and determined fighter it will be once on line. In today's overfished rivers and streams, a fish must be extremely clever to survive from year to year. Chances are, a large brook trout has had several brushes and close calls with both skillful and not-so-skillful anglers. The fish has seen its share of streamers, flies, lures, and hooked baits, and has learned to be more selective in its eating habits. It is also more than likely that a large fish has been hooked at least a few times in its lifetime; it may have even been caught and released by an environmentally conscious angler. Brookies, like all types of trout, learn from their mistakes, and the large ones may know exactly where to swim and what to do to release themselves from the line of a less-than-perfect angler. It is the adaptability of the trout that makes fishing for them such a challenging and enjoyable sport.

While brook trout will quickly strike at a wide variety of baits, they are extremely skittish fish. If a careless angler stomps through the water too loudly or drops his tackle box on the bank, you can rest assured that the brookies in that particular hole will be very wary for at least an hour or two. In shallow, clear streams, where most brook trout live, you should approach the stream very quietly, being careful not to knock anything into the water. Before you start fishing, stand still for a few minutes. Take this time to study the section of stream you will be fishing. Look at where the currents go; where the pools form, and where structures such as large rocks and tree trunks are located on the bottom. If it is a clear stream, you will most likely be able to see the fish on the bottom. Watch them for a while, see where they are holding and what their eating habits are. Study and commit to memory as much of what you see as possible; the information may be invaluable later on.

While many types of tackle, baits, and lures can be used for fishing brookies, the best sport comes from fishing them with a fly. The same holds true when fishing all types of trout. In fact, many of the best trout streams are populated solely by fly anglers, and some have a rule against using any other type of tackle. In many streams, however, it is simply an unspoken rule. If you plop down

The Brook Trout

Trout

The Brook Trout

Left: *The Tetons form a beautiful backdrop for an angler casting for brookies in the Snake River.* Right: *This sleek brook trout fell victim to a Yellow Sally fly. Two other effective flies for brookies are the* Light Cahill *(below left) and the* Quill Gordon *(below right).*

in the middle of a popular trout stream with your spinning rod and a can full of big, juicy nightcrawlers you may catch more dirty looks than brook trout.

Many different factors must be considered in picking the right fly to use in your particular stream on a particular day. You should know what insects, minnows, and larvae are present in the natural environment, what the fish are eating that particular day, what insects are hatching, what season it is, what type of day it is (sunny, cloudy, rainy), and many other "intangible" factors. Choosing a fly to fish with is far from an exact science. One day the fish may be hitting on a size 8 Black Ghost streamer and the next day the same fish may ignore everything but the Grizzly King wet fly. The best advice for novice anglers is to talk to the locals who have been fishing your particular stream for years. Find out what works for them and use that as a starting point in your own fishing. Always carry a wide variety of flies and experiment, experiment, experiment.

Brook trout hit on a range of colorful gaudy wet-fly patterns—the cloudier the day or the murkier the water, the more gaudy the fly they will go for. Some good wet flies to try are: Parmachene Belle, Black Gnat, Royal Coachman, Montreal, Grizzly King, Silver Doctor, and Gray Hackle.

When the brookies are feeding on the surface (usually only during insect hatches in the spring or fall) they may go for dry flies such as the Black Gnat, Light Cahill, Dark Cahill, Royal Coachman, Quill Gordon, Hendrickson, Wulff, and Adams.

Streamers and bucktails are quite effective on brookies. If nothing else is working, you can almost always depend on a Red and White, Mickey Finn, any color Marabou, Edson Tiger, Green or Black Ghost, Black-nosed Dace, or a Muddler Minnow.

While fly anglers are attempting to convert the world to their type of fishing, there are literally hundreds of thousands of anglers who still use a variety of lures and natural baits to catch trout. As stated before, brook trout will strike on almost anything if not startled. Many anglers who use spinning, spin-casting, and bait-casting rods and reels have had great success with a variety of spinners, spoons, jigs, small plugs, and plastic lures. Natural baits such as minnows, grasshoppers, crickets, and nymphs work very well, also, but perhaps nothing compares to fishing with the traditional nightcrawler. Some frustrated fishermen desperate for a fish for their creel have even resorted to using canned corn or pieces of cheese to lure the hungry fish. Brook trout feed primarily on the bottom of the stream, so no matter what bait or lure you are using it is necessary to have a good rig for bottom fishing or drift fishing in order to ensure proper presentation.

The best time of year for catching brook trout is in the early spring, right after the winter snows have thawed. This is when the streams and rivers are running strong with cool, clean, turbulent waters. The fish are very active and voracious eaters at this time, making up for their virtually inactive winter. In most regions, the fishing is best from late March through early June. In northern regions, where the weather stays cool, good fishing can be had through July and August.

As their name implies, brook trout are primarily denizens of small streams and rivers. Brook trout like to hold in moderate currents around and behind submerged logs, boulders, small dams, and other structures as well as in the shade of undercut banks, overhanging trees, and brush. Most of the big brookies will hold in pocket water behind boulders and on the front or back edges of deep pools. In larger streams, however, brook trout will avoid the deep pools, where hungry cutthroat and brown trout may be searching for a big dinner.

In the summer, the fishing tends to fall off a bit, but the brookies are still there and can still be caught if you

The Brook Trout

Trout

This angler (left) has hooked a brook trout in a small mountain stream in Rocky Mountain National Park, Colorado. Above: Another angler waits for a strike on Iron Creek in Wyoming.

The Brook Trout

know where to look for them. Brook trout prefer water that is between 55 and 59°F (13 and 15°C), so as the rivers warm up, they will move upstream to the cooler tributaries. In addition, they will stay primarily on the bottom of the deepest pools and runs and will virtually never come to the surface to feed. In fact, they become so lazy that unless a fly, lure, or bait is dangled directly in front of their nose, they may never strike. During the summer months it is imperative that you go to the brookies, because it is more than likely they will never come to you.

While brook trout are found primarily in streams and rivers, a substantial number live in lakes and large ponds. In the spring, these fish can be found mostly close to shore and around the mouths of brooks and streams entering the lake. As the water warms up, they either swim upstream to the cooler tributaries, or move deeper into the lake. The ones that stay in the lakes live at a depth of between 25 and 50 feet (8 and 16 m), wherever the water is between 55 and 59°F (13 and 15°C). Here, they usually hold around underwater structures, near plateaus, and along drop-offs and ledges.

Around spawning time, male brook trout take on a beautiful reddish hue (left). Female brook trout build shallow redds, or nests (above), in which they deposit anywhere from a few hundred to thousands of eggs.

The Brook Trout

Brook trout spawn in the fall. During these months, they collect at the mouths of cool tributary streams before beginning the trip to their natural spawning grounds. Even though they are more concerned with reproducing than eating, their usual skittishness has been supplanted by the spawning drive, and they are instilled with an uncharacteristic bravado. Brook trout are extremely vulnerable at this time and will strike at virtually anything they see. Many conservation-minded anglers, who are concerned about the future of the brook trout, will not fish for them during the spawning season. If you do fish during the brookies' spawning period, always release the drably colored females and handle them with extreme care.

Most spawning occurs in the small headwater streams where the fish construct redds (shallow depositories) in the loose gravel on the stream bottom. An average-sized female fish will deposit anywhere from a few hundred to thousands of eggs, which will hatch anytime from thirty-five to 140 days, depending on the water temperature. While the spawning and hatching characteristics of brook trout are similar to those of the salmon, they don't partake in the same spectacular life-or-death runs as salmon.

The future of the brook trout in North America—the United States especially—is very tenuous. There are currently few surviving natural populations. Small underfished streams in remote sections of the Northeast and the Rocky Mountain states as well as in eastern Canada, are about the only places where brook trout still breed naturally. Stocking operations, however, have been very successful, and literally hundreds of thousands of "farm-fed" brook trout are released, and subsequently caught, every year. Yet, if North American streams and rivers continue to be victimized by industrial pollution and acid rain, even stocked fish will not be able to survive long enough to be fished.

Chapter 3

Rainbow trout

It is a sunny, yet brisk, early spring day. The ice and snow from the long winter have recently melted and the rivers and streams are running cold and fast. It is the opening of trout season, the time of year when anglers, with rod and reel in hand, descend upon rivers and streams across North America by the bus loads. Whether they are spinning, bait-casting, or fly-fishing, their goals are the same: to enjoy the rehabilitating effects of the cool mountain air and to catch some lean, hungry trout.

Clearly, anglers are happy to reel in any type of trout—brookies, browns, cutthroats—yet perhaps the most popular, sought-after, and visually spectacular of all strains is the *Salmo gairdneri*, or more popularly, the rainbow trout. As its name implies, the rainbow has a distinctive veneer of color and markings. Its back is a metallic blue or green, which shades into a more silvery green on its sides. The fish is dotted with dark spots all along the top, sides, head, and dorsal and caudal fins. Its belly is usually a silvery white. The most spectacular marking on the rainbow is the wide band of crimson or pink running along the lateral line of the fish from gills to tail. The rainbow's dots and slash of crimson are usually more pronounced in males during the spawning season.

The rainbow is a native of western North America, whose natural range goes from the Bering Sea to Southern

Rainbow Trout

Opposite page: This angler displays a large rainbow he caught with a Royal Wulff Fly. The Stony Creek (left) in Six Rivers National Forest, California, offers some excellent trout fishing.

California. In fresh water, its range is primarily in lakes and streams in the western regions of North America bordering the Pacific Ocean from Alaska down through British Columbia and the United States to Baja California. While the rainbow is solely a western native, huge populations of the fish have been introduced in suitable waters throughout Canada and the United States. The vast majority of the rainbows caught in the East are "stockers," although several natural populations have formed in clean, cool inland streams that are not overfished. In coastal streams, most stocked rainbows are either caught or eventually make their way out to sea.

In small streams and lakes, rainbows average between 1 and 6 pounds (1/3 to 2 kg), with big lunkers weighing in at about 8 pounds (3 kg). In larger bodies of water, they can grow as big as 15 to 20 pounds (7 to 9 kg)—enough fish to feed a small family. Most of these large trout are found in Ontario, British Columbia, and western states such as Idaho. The largest variety of rainbow trout is the Kamloops rainbow, which is

This fly angler nets a rainbow in the swift-flowing Gibbon River of Wyoming. Rainbows love the strong currents of fast-moving streams and rivers.

found mostly in British Columbia. Kamloops of 30 pounds (11 kg) and more have been caught with a rod and a reel in Jewel Lake, British Columbia, and specimens as big as 52 pounds (19 kg) have been caught in nets by game wardens.

There are two distinct strains of rainbow trout: the steelhead and the McCloud. Similar to the salmon, the steelhead carries a migratory instinct to go out to sea, where it matures and then returns to fresh water to spawn. These seagoing rainbows are far less colorful than the freshwater McCloud. They have different characteristics and, therefore, require different fishing techniques. Because of these differences, steelhead will be discussed separately in a later chapter.

When most anglers think of rainbow trout, they think of the McCloud. These freshwater fish love the strong currents of fast-moving streams and rivers. They can usually be found holding around the edges of rapids, riffles, and small pockets. Some of their favorite holding spots are in the heads or tails of pools around white-

Rainbow Trout

Trout

Opposite page: *A feisty rainbow trout may jump several times before finally tiring.* Right: *This fish was caught using a small spinner.* Below, left to right: *Royal Coachman and Black Gnat are two good dry-fly patterns when the rainbows are hitting the surface.*

water areas. Many fishermen avidly fish for rainbows under waterfalls or at the feet of small dams, where the water is running strong. While these fish love strong currents, they usually do not lie in the strongest sections of the streams. They congregate around the edges of the fastest-moving water, behind rocks, sunken logs, and fallen trees. In the early morning and evening hours big rainbows feed in shallow, fast-moving water. As the sun heats up the stream in midday, however, they usually retreat to the cooler pools and drop-offs, and into the shade of overhanging trees and carved-out riverbanks.

Many anglers use a wide variety of natural baits for pulling in rainbows by the armful. Salmon eggs, crawfish, grubs, minnows, and the traditional nightcrawler fished on or near the bottom all work well on rainbows. In a growing number of areas, however, bait fishing for rainbows and other trout is now illegal due to the depletion of fish populations from pollution and overfishing. In some other areas, where bait fishing is still officially allowed, it is not generally accepted by the fishing public. Many an ardent fly fisher will look down on the bait fisherman as a hack or a poacher. Clearly, the method of choice is quickly becoming fly fishing.

While rainbows are primarily bottom feeders, they will rise for a dry fly during heavy insect hatches. Many anglers maintain that fishing for rainbows with a dry fly provides the purest sport. Dry-fly fishing can be an exacting science that requires a great deal of experimentation, knowledge of the river, familiarity with the fish's feeding habits, and sometimes complicated casting and retrieving techniques. The secret is in matching the dry fly with the insects that are hatching at that time in a particular location, and then presenting the fly in a natural way. Like most trout, rainbows are extremely skittish fish and will not hit on something that does not act naturally or looks artificial.

While it is necessary to match your dry fly with each individual fishing situation, a few good patterns to start with include Hendrickson, Black Gnat, Ginger Quill, Royal Coachman, Quill Gordon, Grizzly Sedge, and Green Sedge. Certain salmon flies can also be effective, particularly in western waters.

Even the most ardent and successful fishermen do not rely solely on dry flies. If they did, there would be times when they would never even get a strike. Because rainbows are such voracious bottom feeders, wet flies, nymphs, streamers, and bucktails are all extremely effective. All of these flies should be fished close to the bottom using sinking line and leader. If you are fishing in fast-moving deep water, it may even be necessary to add a small, split-shot sinker or piece of lead tape to your line. Be careful, however, not to add too much weight or it will impede casting with the fly rod and alter the natural drift of the fly.

The Stonefly (below left) and the Red Squirrel (below right) are two effective fly patterns for snagging rainbows, while the Johnson Silver Minnow (middle) is an excellent lure. Rainbow trout love to forage for food in the strong currents of cool mountain streams. Once hooked, they will immediately head downstream and try to snag your line on a fallen tree or submerged rock. Here, (opposite page) an angler plays a recently hooked rainbow while a friend looks on.

Some good wet flies to have on hand include Royal Coachman, Alexandria, both Brown and Green Sedges, Black Gnat, Woolly Worm, Parmachene Bell, Skykomish Sunrise, and both Gray and Yellow Hackle.

Nymphs will most likely be the fly of choice for fishing rainbows in shallow, clear rivers and small lakes and ponds. Some good nymph patterns include Montana Nymph, Gridlebug, Brown Stonefly, Black Stonefly, and Box Canyon Stone.

On days when you've tried just about every dry fly, wet fly, or nymph you own, it seems you can always fall back on a few good bucktails or streamers to ensure a hit. Bucktails and streamers are long, feathery, hairy flies primarily intended to imitate minnows and small fish. They are drifted along the bottom and can be especially effective in deep or murky water. While it is not necessary to have a huge variety of streamers and bucktails in your tackle box, it is good to have a few different sizes and colors for use in various fishing situations. As a general rule for all types of flies, it is better to use more colorful flies in murky water or on cloudy days, and more plain, drably colored flies when the water is clear. But remember, no rule in fishing holds true all the time. In fact, many times the exceptions yield better results than the most tried-and-true methods.

Some good bucktails and streamers to have on hand for landing a finicky rainbow include Black Ghost, Black Marabou, Yellow Marabou, Red Squirrel Gold, Mickey Finn, Brown Bucktail, Warden's Worry, Woolly Bugger, and Muddler Minnow.

In most areas, rainbow fishing is best in the early spring right after the snow melts and the rivers and streams are running cold and fast. This is when the larger rainbows begin their trek upstream to spawn. The best springtime fishing takes place in late March, April, and early to mid-May, depending, of course, on how long the water stays cool in a given area. During the early spring months—and to a lesser extent in the late fall—some of the best fishing can be had in the middle of the day, when the fish are extremely active. At this time, rainbows can be found in the fast currents bordering fallen trees, large rocks, or next to undercut banks. Even though there may be a lot of hungry fish in a particular stretch of stream, rainbow trout are extremely selective in their eating habits and will not go out of their way to chase a bait or a fly.

If the fish are feeding on the bottom, as they do most of the year, it is best to use a wet fly, nymph, or streamer. Stand upstream about 60 feet (18 m) from where you think the rainbows are holding and wait several minutes to settle any skittish fish who may have seen your approach. Cast across stream and up at about a forty-five-degree angle from where you are standing. Let the fly sink and drift naturally downstream with the current, keeping the line taut enough so that you can feel a strike, but not so taut that it inhibits the drift of the fly. As the fly drifts past you, begin slowly letting out line so that it can drift downstream to the intended hole. As the fly reaches the hole, stop letting out line. The fly will hold for a few seconds and then begin to slowly drift back across stream. Be alert, because this is when you will get most of your strikes. If you feel even the slightest tug on the line, lift the tip of rod with a quick jerk to set the hook. Chances are, it was a false alarm—a snag or the fly drifting on the bottom—but if you don't try to set the hook, you may miss your fish.

If no fish strikes at this point, let the fly begin to drift across stream and begin a slow retrieve, employing quick, short, jerky movements on the line. Do not, however, retrieve the line too quickly. Many a fish has been missed by an impatient angler who is anxious to make another cast. You can't catch any fish when your line is not in the water. In addition, don't give up on a particular spot just because you make several casts without a hit. Experiment using different flies and different retrieves and most importantly, fish each section of stream well; if the fish are there, chances are they will eventually hit on something.

This angler casts for rainbows on the Firehole River in Yellowstone National Park, as the Bison look on in the background.

As the summer sun begins to warm the waters in the months of June, July, and August, the fishing often slows down. During these months, most of the larger rainbows will attempt to escape the heat by moving to the cooler lakes and large pools. Those fish that remain in the streams will be found almost exclusively in fast water, except in the early morning or evening, when they may search small pools and deeper waters for minnows. Some of the best summer fishing you can find can be had in small pools right at daybreak using either bucktail and streamer flies or small spinning lures.

When going for the larger rainbows in lakes or deep pools, it is best to use weighted wet flies and nymphs fished deep with a sinking line. Rainbows are very particular about their water temperature. They normally like the water to be between 55 and 60°F (13 and 15°C) and will not eat if the water is too cool or too warm. As a result, lake rainbows will usually stay at a particular depth during the summer. If you can find the depth where they are feeding, you will be in for some

Trout

Once hooked, the rainbow can put up a very determined fight. Opposite page: This angler enjoys an early morning fishing session on Leigh Lake in the Grand Tetons National Park, Wyoming.

very productive fishing. Cast your line out and let the fly sink, taking note as to how deep the fly goes on each cast. Retrieve the fly with short, quick pulls; it is during your retrieve that you will get the most strikes. Experiment with different depths until you get a few strikes, and then continue fishing that depth until it ceases to be productive. If you are having trouble getting your fly to sink to the proper depth, add a small split-shot sinker or a piece of lead tape to your leader.

Spinning lures and small spoons are also very effective for catching lake rainbows. The fishing method here is similar to deep fishing with wet flies, except that the retrieve may be done with slightly longer pulls to impart the proper spinning motion on the lure. Some effective spinners include Al's Goldfish, Gold Kastmaster, and the Yellow Rooster Tail.

Still another effective method for catching lake rainbows is plunking. This simply entails placing a natural bait on a weighted rig, casting out into the lake, placing the rod on a Y-shaped stick or a log, and sitting

Rainbow Trout

back and enjoying the day until a fish hits. If a school of hungry rainbows comes into the area, "plunkers" may be able to pull fish out as quickly as they can cast.

One of the most popular methods for fishing rainbows in large rivers is from a small boat or canoe. Many a relaxing and enjoyable day can be whiled away sitting in a rowboat in the middle of a river, casting for rainbows and other fish. The best method for boat fishing is to anchor the canoe or boat about 60 feet (18 m) upstream from where you believe the fish are holding. Then simply let your lure or bait drift downstream at about 20 feet (6 m) at a time, holding for a few minutes between each interval. Once the line reaches the hole, let it stay there for a few minutes and then begin jerking in and letting it drift back. If you don't get a hit in about five to ten minutes, begin pulling it in using short rhythmic movements. If you do get hit but don't land the fish, remember

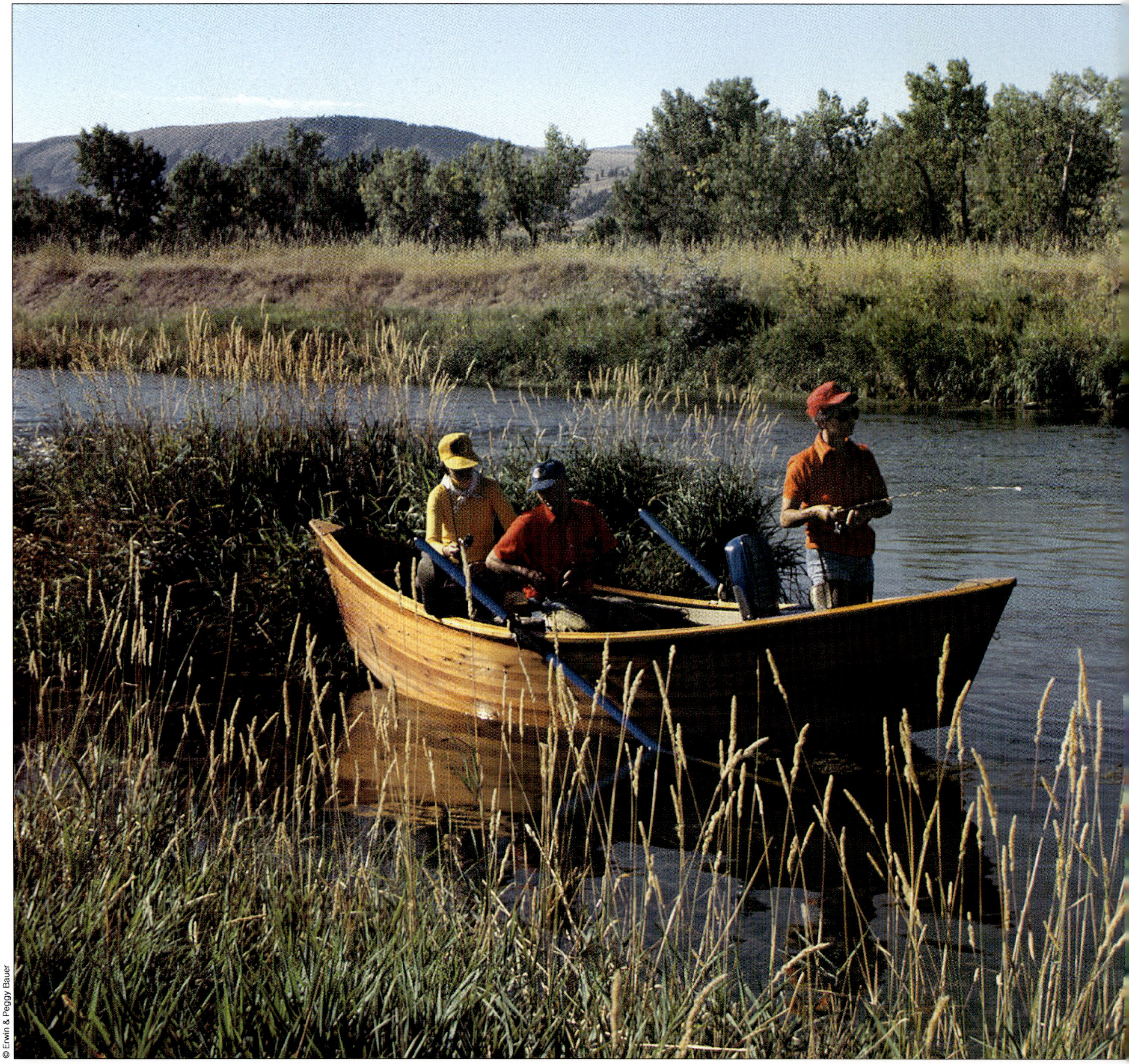

© Erwin & Peggy Bauer

Rainbow Trout

When fishing from a boat, it is important to anchor or drift the boat at least 60 feet (28 m) from where you believe the fish are sitting. These anglers are float-fishing down the Bighorn River in Montana.

where in the river the hit came and what movement you were putting on the lure. Repeat that action and see if a fish will hit again. It is important to experiment using different movement and retrieving techniques. If the fish are there you will eventually hit on something that works. Never give up on a spot too soon. Many a fish has been missed by an impatient fisherman.

Rainbows are perhaps the most widespread of all North American game fish. While they are originally natives of the West, they are highly adaptive fish that have been successfully transplanted into streams, rivers, and lakes all over the United States and Canada. The largest rainbows in the world are still found in British Columbia; however, some extremely large fish have been pulled from the waters of Argentina, Chile, Peru, Australia, and New Zealand. In the United States, the largest rainbows are found in Washington, Oregon, northern California, Idaho, Utah, Montana, Michigan, Wisconsin, Minnesota, and New York.

Chapter 4

Steelhead

It is winter at the Skykomish River in Washington State. The air is damp and cold and the water is running strong from long December rains. Up near the headwaters of this scenic river, resourceful anglers brace

Trout

Steelhead can fight with rod-bending ferocity, as is evident in this photo (opposite page) of an angler battling a steelie on the Coquille River in Oregon. Even when netted, steelhead may continue to thrash about.

themselves against the cold, harsh winds as they line the banks with rod and reel in hand. They are eager to test their skills against one of the fiercest fighting fish of North America. It is the great winter run of the steelhead trout (*Salmo gairdneri*).

Each winter, thousands of these mighty fish desperately fight their way from the Pacific Ocean upstream to their original birthplace. Here they spawn, laying their eggs in "redds" constructed in the gravelly stream floor. They will never see the product of their efforts, because after spawning they only pause long enough to regain their strength before turning around and heading back out to sea.

By the middle of April, the tiny steelhead offspring will begin pushing their way out of the gravel. Here they will stay and grow until their own genetic code takes over and drives them downstream to the Pacific Ocean. Once at sea, the young steelhead will lose their colorful markings for the silver-blue of ocean fish. For two years or more, the steelhead migrate through the endless feeding grounds of the ocean, growing large and strong. Then suddenly an instinctual alarm clock goes off, and these now-powerful fish return to the river and make their way back to the spawning grounds, just as their parents did before them.

The steelhead trout is actually a strain of rainbow trout that carries the instinct to migrate to sea. In fact, when in fresh water, the steelhead retains the same colorful markings as the rainbow. After going to sea, however, the steelhead quickly loses its coloring and becomes bigger, longer, and more streamlined than the rainbow. While in the ocean the steelhead has a steel-blue or greenish back, silvery sides, and dark spots on its back and tail. The steelhead gets its name from its coloring as well as from its extremely strong skull, which, according to fishing lore, forced net fishermen to administer several blows from a club to kill the fish when brought on the boat.

The largest run of steelheads takes place during the winter months;

In large rivers and lakes, many anglers fish for steelheads from boats, either by casting or trolling. While this type of fishing is not quite as exciting as casting from shore or wading in the water, it can still yield some very sizable results.

however, some are usually running every month of the year, with the second largest run taking place during the summer. Winter steelhead are also by far the largest of the strain, sometimes reaching 15 to 20 pounds (6 to 8 kg). Summer steelhead, by contrast, usually top out at about 8 pounds (3 kg). The record catch for steelhead is a 42-pound (16-kg) monster caught by David White on June 22, 1970, in Alaska.

The steelhead's natural range is from Alaska to northern California, with some of the best fishing taking place in the cool rivers of British Columbia, Washington, and Oregon. Once at sea, these resourceful fish can sometimes migrate for hundreds of miles. In 1972, several hundred steelhead were tagged around the Aleutian Islands. Two years later, a few of them were caught in the rivers of Washington State. More commonly, however, these traveling fish stay well within one hundred miles (160 km) of the entrance to their spawning river.

Next to the Pacific salmon, the steelhead is probably the most popular game fish among experienced West Coast anglers. On the East Coast, by contrast, steelhead fishing is virtually nonexistent. Many of the stocked rainbows in the East do make their way to the ocean, but they do not carry the strong migratory and spawning instincts of the western steelhead. There are a few steelhead stocking operations in the Great Lakes area; however, natural reproduction has not been very successful.

Much of their popularity comes from the steelhead's large size and extremely strong fighting ability. When you get a strike from a steelhead you will know it. They hit hard and fast and fight with a dogged deter-

TROUT

Like the salmon, steelhead trout make life-or-death runs upstream to their spawning waters. This steelie is desperately trying to jump past the Winchester Dam in southern Oregon.

mination. Steelies of all sizes make long, powerful runs, taking your line downstream through swift-running water. Sometimes they run for 150 feet (46 m) or more while viciously tugging and shaking their heads like a pit bull with a piece of raw meat. They dart around sharp rocks and fallen trees in hopes of breaking your line, most times with great success. You can consider yourself as having a good day if you can land 50 percent of the steelies you hook.

Perhaps the most spectacular parts of the steelhead's run are its dramatic, arched-back breaches. An extremely feisty steelie may jump four or five times in a single run.

There is nothing more exhilarating than seeing a 10-pound (4-kg) fish at the end of your line, hurdling completely out of the water with its head and tail flailing in the breeze and then splashing back down and continuing its run. It will literally raise bumps on your flesh.

The first key to success in fishing for steelhead is being able to find them. In certain areas, steelhead runs may vary from river to river and from year to year. Most rivers have two major runs, one during the winter and one during the summer. Yet even this is just a rough guideline. The brunt of the run may occur during different months from year to year, depending on weather, currents, and certain other ambiguous factors. There are many rivers in Washington and British Columbia that have more or less continuous runs throughout the year.

If you are planning a trip to catch steelhead, you are well advised to do a little research before finalizing your plans. Contact local fish and game authorities and area fishing stores to find out about the runs and local fishing conditions. On longer rivers, the runs are usually spread out through a season; however, different sections

Steelhead are one of the most popular game fish in western North America. Below: An angler displays a fish he caught in the Bogachiel River, Washington. Right: Another angler nets a steelhead from a river in Alaska. Opposite page: A tireless angler casts after steelies on the Queets River in Washington.

of the river are productive at different times as the fish move upstream. If you are lucky enough to live near a steelhead river, make several trips simply to observe the fish. Find out when they feed, where their holding spots are, and how long the run lasts. The more you know about the fish you are going for, the better your chances of fishing success.

It is also wise to continually check weather reports around a potential river. A prolonged rain or sudden storm may cloud the water and put fishing at a standstill for days or even weeks. Most steelhead will not feed when the water level rises quickly and becomes murky. Once the river clears, however, fishing will again become productive. Keep in mind that the headwaters and small tributary streams clear much faster than the lower portions of the river.

If you are fishing the winter run, keep an eye out for sudden temperature drops. Steelies become inactive and do very little feeding when the water becomes extremely cold. Generally, if the water temperature stays above 39°F (4°C), the fishing will be good. On particularly cold days, your best luck will most likely come during the afternoons after the water warms up a bit.

As steelhead move upstream to their spawning grounds, they tend to lie in several different holding spots along the way. These "rest stops" are usually protected from the strongest

Trout

Whether you are fishing with a fly outfit (opposite page) or a spinning outfit (right), steelhead provide ample excitement and challenge for even the most experienced of anglers. Below: The Gooey Bob by Luhr Jensen, which imitates a salmon egg cluster, is an excellent lure for running steelhead.

currents. Steelhead hold around the edges of fast waters or at the heads or tails of riffles and runs. Like other trout, they are structure lovers. Look for them around boulders, sunken tree trunks, carved-out banks, and rock ledges. Steelhead also hold around the edges of large pools, although they very seldom go in the deepest section of a pool.

Once you find one of these rest stops, you should be in for some exciting fishing. Anglers use a wide variety of outfits when fishing for steelies—everything from ultralight fly rods, to heavy surf fishing rods. For years, the outfit of choice was a 6½- to 8½-foot (2- to 3-m) spinning rod with a small spinning reel filled with 9- to 15-pound (3- to 6-kg) test line. Silver, gold, and brass spoons in various weights and sizes usually work well in the steelies' fast-moving rivers. Some of the most successful lures are imitation salmon egg clusters such as the Oakie Drifter and the Spin and Glo, as well as wobblers such as the Lil Jasper and Fat Max and cherry bombers such as Luhr Jensen Fireplug and Prism Glo.

When fishing steelhead with a lure, you must drift the lure along the bottom fast enough so that you can actually feel the action of the spinner blade. The tricky part is in fishing close to the bottom and around obstacles without getting your hook snagged. With practice, you will better understand the feel of your rod and the action of your lure, and snags will become less prevalent. If snagging becomes a major problem you may want to replace the treble hook on your lure with a single hook. Also, be sure to have several lures with your tackle. You are sure to lose at least a few on the bottom.

As you fish a certain section of river, study it well. Take mental note of where obstacles are, where the currents flow, where the pools form, and most importantly, where the fish are holding. The longer you fish the same hole, the better you will become at guiding your lure in and around pools and obstacles, taking it right to the fish's mouth. If it is an extremely productive hole, try to commit as much of it to memory as you can. You may even consider writing down a few notes about it before you leave. That way, if you return to that hole on a day when the water is deeper or less clear, you will still have a good idea where the obstacles are and where the fish are holding.

The best natural bait for catching steelhead is a handmade egg cluster or a fresh roe sack. Egg clusters can be bought in a jar at most fishing stores or you can make your own using fresh roe. To do this, you place the eggs in the center of a small square of nylon netting. Gather the corners of the netting together and tie them with a piece of thin thread. Other good natural baits include

Trout

Below: *Salmon eggs, when clustered with a small piece of nylon netting, make a good natural bait for steelhead trout. Even though steelhead do not generally eat while on their spawning run, they will instinctively go after salmon eggs.*

crawfish tails, nightcrawlers, and minnows (where legal). The most traditional bait-fishing rig is still the most effective and easiest to handle. Tie a three-way swivel to the end of your line. To the top eyelet of the swivel tie 2 to 3 feet (.6 to .9m) of 8-pound (3-kg) test monofilament leader with a hook at the end. To the lower eyelet tie a 4- to 6-inch (15-cm) piece of 4-pound (2-kg) test (or lower) leader with a sinker attached. It is best to use a pencil sinker, because it will be less likely to snag. If it does snag, however, you will be able to

White choppy water areas, such as this, are prime spots for snagging running steelhead.

break it off easily because of the weakness of the sinker leader. Simply give a short, hard tug on the line and the sinker should break away easily.

The method for fishing with live bait is slightly different from fishing with a lure or a wet fly. Position yourself directly downstream from where the fish are holding. Cast the bait 30 to 40 feet (9 to 12 m) above the hole and let it sink to nearly the bottom. Be extremely careful with your cast when fishing with this method. If you come up short on a cast, you will startle the fish and ruin your chances. Inexperienced anglers who are not confident in their casting ability should consider fishing from upstream and letting the bait drift down past the fishing hole. As the bait begins to roll with the current, keep the rod tip low and take in just enough line to control the bait. If you have too much slack you will not be able to feel a strike. When the method is working properly you will be able to feel the sinker bouncing along the bottom. You should respond with a sharp tug at even the indication of a strike.

Trout

Below: *The Skykomish Sunrise (right) and the Light Umpqua Special (left) are two excellent flies for catching steelhead.* Right: *The Trinity River in California is one of the many western rivers to offer good steelhead fishing.*

While fishing steelhead with lures and natural baits remains extremely popular, the real sport comes in catching these mighty fighters on a fly rod. The most popular outfit is an 8- to 9½-foot (2- to 3-m) graphite or bamboo fly rod loaded with slow-sinking or medium-sinking fly line. Because steelhead are primarily bottom feeders, wet flies and streamers are most effective. A few good patterns include: Royal Coachman, Silver Ant, Thor, Gray Hackle, Skykomish, Cummings, Umpqua, Silver Demons, Van Luven, Queen Bess, Harger's Orange, Fire Fly, Burlap, and Kalama Special.

The most common method for fishing steelhead with a fly is to cast across and slightly upstream, letting the fly sink and drift downstream into the prospective hole. Another somewhat more complicated method is to cast across and slightly downstream. As soon as the fly touches the water, begin to dip and raise the rod tip once every five seconds with a slow and rhythmic movement. As you do this, strip in about a handful of line at a time. You should strip in a total of about two to three feet of line during the entire drift. Let the fly drift downstream until it begins to work its way back across stream, continuing the rhythmic motion. Once it gets about three-quarters of the way across stream, begin a slow retrieval.

It is important that your fly is sinking properly. If it doesn't sink properly after the first cast, soak it well before casting again. Some anglers even go so far as to dip their fly in mud to make it sink quickly. If your fly still isn't sinking properly, consider changing to a quicker-sinking line and leader, or add a small split-shot sinker to your line.

Opposite page: The Smith River in Six Rivers National Forest, California, comes alive during the run of the steelhead trout.

Steelhead Rivers

British Columbia	Fraser, Kispiox, Cowichan, Skeena, Cooper, Sustut, Vedder, Thompson, Beela Coola, Babine, and Dean
California	Guatuala, Trinity, Sacramento, American, Russian, Feather, Smith, Yuba, Klamath, and Matole
Oregon	Columbia, Wilson, Sandy, Alsea, Destuches, Coquille, Siletz, Umpqua, Rogue, Siuslaw, and Big Nestucca
Washington	Duckabush, Toutle, Kalama, Willapa, Stillaguamish, Nooksack, Snoqualmie, Bogachiel, Washougal, Naselle, Wind, Queets, Quinault, Rogue, Dosewallips, Wenatchee, Green, Puyallup, Lewis, Cowlitz, Skagit, Chehalis, Skykomish, and Nisqually

When fighting a big steelhead with a fly rod, don't attempt to strip in line with your hand. You will have greater success playing the fish with the reel. Steelies are extremely able fighters and will break loose with even the slightest kink or misplay. Let the steelie take out line and tire itself; however, try to keep it from running through obstacles or into fast-running water. Landing a steelhead takes a great deal of skill and more than a small amount of patience. Once hooked, they will immediately start to swim downstream heading straight for white water. While you do want to try to carefully guide the fish away from white water and other sharp obstacles, if you attempt to reel it in too soon, you will most assuredly lose the fish.

At certain times during the late summer and early fall, steelhead will feed on insects hatching on the surface. During these big insect hatches dry flies can be extremely effective. A few good dry-fly patterns to use for steelies include Gray Wulff, Black Wulff, Steelhead Bee, and Surface Stonefly.

Steelhead offer some of the most challenging and exciting sport fishing in North America. For the novice, however, those first few steelhead trips may be extremely frustrating. You will most likely lose fish after fish, while leaving your share of tackle on the river floor. Every outing will be a learning experience as you get to know the ins and outs of your equipment and the determined fighting characteristics of the savvy steelhead. Even the most experienced anglers can be frustrated by these feisty ocean-run fish. That is why they return to the swift rivers of Oregon, Washington, and British Columbia year after year, and suffer through often miserably cold conditions of the winter steelhead run.

Steelhead

Chapter 5

© Jeff March/Photo/Nats

Brown Trout

While it is estimated that the brown trout has been around for more than 70 million years, it did not appear on the North American continent until near the end of the nineteenth century. In 1882, William

Gilbert of Plymouth, Massachusetts, imported the first five thousand eggs of this European native. Unfortunately, the vast majority of the eggs proved infertile and failed to hatch, and from those eggs that did hatch, only three fry ever grew to spawning age. Yet, those three fish marked the beginning of the brown trout fishery in North America.

Less than one year later, a German named Herr F. Von Behr sent eighty thousand eggs to Fred Mather of the Cold Spring Harbor Hatchery on Long Island, New York. These eggs fared much better. Some of them were forwarded to the United States Fish Commission's hatchery in Northville, Michigan, and the remainder were sent to the Caledonia hatchery in New York State. Tens of thousands of fish were raised, spawned, and their offspring released into the prime trout waters of North America. Over the next few years, more shipments of brown trout eggs were sent from Scotland, Ireland, England, and Germany. The initial distribution of the brown was centered primarily in New York State

Brown Trout

Opposite page: A staff member looks over the tanks at a fish hatchery in Thompson, Michigan. Below: These two browns were caught using an antique bamboo fly rod.

waters; however, by 1900 the fish had been introduced in thirty-eight states and throughout much of Canada. Today, the brown trout is present in virtually every viable trout stream in North America.

The brown trout, or *Salmo trutta*, is a moderately compressed, elongate fish that ranges from pale yellow to olive brown on its back and sides. Its colors become lighter toward its belly, which is a silvery white. Its body is marked with numerous red or orange spots surrounded by halos. As browns become older and larger they lose some of their markings and they develop big heads and hooked jaws. Sea-run browns and those that live in large lakes also lose some of their colorings and markings and tend to turn bright silver.

At one time, scientists used to differentiate between the various strains of brown—European brown, German brown, Loch Levens—however, hybridization of the fish in North America has made such distinctions obsolete to all but the piscatorial purists.

The brownie spawns anytime between September and December, depending on the geographic area it is found and the weather in that area. The female of the species digs a shallow hole in the gravelly stream bottom and deposits her eggs. Both the eggs and the newly hatched fry are vulnerable to predators such as crawfish and minnows. It is estimated that as many as 80 percent of all eggs and fry are eaten or destroyed before reaching maturity. Yet, despite this, the *Salmo trutta* continues to thrive.

The brown was an extremely unpopular fish when it was first introduced in North America. Originally dubbed "the speckled carp," the brown was accused of being ugly, unappetizing, and a poor fighter. In addition, anglers complained that the brown was responsible for the disappearance of other, more desirable trout, such as the brookie. This

Many conservation-minded anglers practice catch-and-release fishing. Here an angler gently releases a brown back to the Beaverkill in New York.

latter accusation is at least partially true. Like all trout, the brown is a cannibal that feeds on other, smaller trout. In addition, it is a very aggressive and territorial fish. One large, old brown trout will stake claim to a stretch of stream and drive away any other fish that attempt to intrude.

While the brown trout may not be the hardest fighting of all the trouts, it is nonetheless the most difficult to catch. It is an extremely wary and adaptable fish that quickly learns how to survive in hard-fished streams and rivers. In addition, browns can withstand relatively high levels of pollution. So as civilization encroaches and brookies and rainbows die out in increasingly warm, acid-rain-stricken streams, only the brown trout may remain.

The brown's aggressiveness and adaptability have made it a very good fish for stocking programs. They are easy fish to raise and quickly form natural populations once released in the wild. Unfortunately, this can sometimes spell doom for other types of fish. In order to compensate for overly successful brown stocking programs, a few fish and game commissions have put higher bag limits on browns than on rainbows, cutthroats, and brooks. This, however, has only been partially successful. Since browns are so difficult to catch, the majority fall victim only to highly skilled fly anglers, who very seldom keep anything they catch. Rainbows and brooks, on the other hand, are sought after by the average angler who is looking for good food for the table.

While the brown trout is still not very popular among casual or novice anglers, it is perhaps the most highly regarded of all fish among fly fishers and dry-fly purists. Ever since seventeenth-century author Sir Izaak Walton poetically sang the praises of the brown trout in the fishing classic, *The Compleat Angler* [sic], fly enthusiasts of all walks of life have eagerly tried to match wits with the wily brown. This highly intelligent fish has excellent senses of sight, smell, and hearing. In addition, it can see extremely well in dim light and has the uncanny ability to focus on two objects at the same time. If the angler's fly does not closely resemble the fish's natural quarry in both appearance and action, the brownie will not give it a second look. Making matters even more difficult, the brownie may not feed on the same insect, minnow, or small fish from one day to the next, and very seldom will it venture very far out of its lair to take even the most appetizing of lures.

Volumes upon volumes have been written on the art (or science?) of matching the fly to fish's natural food. These tomes range from highly academic, scientific studies to the experiences of tried-and-true anglers, to fishing myth, to simple intuition. Yet, no matter how many books and studies may be put forth on the subject, the brown trout continues to be a worthy adversary to even the most seasoned anglers.

When challenging the brown with the fly rod, it is essential to have a good selection of dry, wet, nymph, and streamer fly patterns on hand. More than any other trout, the brown will rise to the surface to feed, particularly during heavy insect hatches. During these times, dry-fly fishing is the method of choice. Getting a big,

Fly Patterns for the Brown Trout

Dry Flies	Royal Wulff (or any other dry fly in the Wulff series), Royal Coachman, Ginger Quill, Light Blue Quill, Quill Gordon, Red Quill, Adams, Hendrickson, Black Gnat, Pale Evening Dun, Blue Dun, Goofus Bug
Midges (gnatlike fly)	Blue Dun Midge, Brown Midge, Black Midge, and Olive Midge
Terrestrials	Black Ant, Crowe Beetle, Inchworm, Letort Hopper, Letort Cricket, Deer Hopper, Michigan Hopper, and Jassid
Wet Flies	Dave's Sculpin, Zug Bug, Woolly Worm, March Brown, Ginger Quill, Leadwig Coachman, Hendrickson, Deer Fly, Catskill, Grizzly King, and Pale Evening Dun
Nymphs	Brown Stonefly, March Brown, Ted's Stonefly, Caddis Larva, Gray Nymph, Hare's Ear, and Dragon
Streamers	Muddler Minnow, White Marabou, Black Marabou, Gray Ghost, Black Ghost, Golden Darter, Grizzly King, and Mickey Finn

© Alan L. Detrick

Brown Trout

Below: The brown trout will rise to the fly more readily than virtually any other game fish. Right: The inchworm is one of the many terrestrials effective against the brown trout.

old brown trout to rise to a dry fly is perhaps the greatest accomplishment of a fly angler. The choice of fly and method of presentation will depend greatly on what particular insects are hatching at any given time. In addition to insect hatches, browns will feed on the surface in the summer on terrestrial insects that fall into the water. There is a wide variety of fly patterns designed to imitate crickets, grasshoppers, beetles, and ants. The majority of the time, however, browns feed under the surface, so it is necessary to have a good selection of wet flies, nymphs, and streamers on hand as well. The chart on page 86 is a guide to a variety of fly patterns that have historically been successful against the brown trout. This, however, is just a starting point. You can never really have too many flies in your collection. When fishing a particular area, ask the advice of local fishermen, fishing store owners, and fish and game commissions. The knowledge they possess may be invaluable.

The first step in catching browns is knowing where they are. As stated

A couple of anglers and a friend fly fish from a boat on Henry's Fork, Snake River, Idaho.

earlier, browns are very territorial fish that won't usually venture too far out of their lair to feed. This is particularly true of large browns. As long as the food supply holds out in their particular stretch of stream, they may only leave to spawn or to chase intruding fish away. If you come across a stretch of an otherwise productive trout stream that seems barren of fish, chances are it is the home of a lone, old, hook-jawed lunker. Make no mistake, this fish knows its territory well and will hold in the most obstruction-filled part of the stream. In addition, an age-old brownie has seen its share of flies presented in a wide variety of ways and won't be easily fooled. And even when hooked, browns are veritable experts at snagging lines and breaking free. If you are an extremely patient, determined, and highly skilled angler you may want to try to match wits with this venerable *piscis;* however, your time may be more productively spent searching for a stretch of stream where more numerous (if smaller) browns may be found.

Brown trout are sensitive to light and thus like to hold in deep water under and around brush, fallen trees, large rocks, undercut banks, and bridges. They can usually be found around the edges of the main current, where the oxygen is plentiful and the food is carried directly to them. They do not like strong current and will hold behind a rock or another obstruction that splits the flow of the water.

It is wise to spend a substantial amount of time studying the stream or river before starting to fish. If you live nearby, visit the stream several times simply to see where the fish hold and what their feeding habits are. If you are not so lucky, devote half an hour to an hour to study. A good pair of polarized sunglasses is an invaluable tool for observing fish. Remember, however, that the brown trout, even more so than other types of trout, is an extremely skittish fish. Loud noises or unusual shadows on the water may spook the fish and ruin your chances for catching it for at least a few hours and maybe the entire day.

Brown Trout

A hopeful angler casts into a beaver pond in Rocky Mountain National Park, Colorado.

When insects are hatching in and around the stream, you will most likely notice small splashes dotting the water surface as the hungry browns come up for lunch. This is the time for dry-fly fishing. As stated earlier, matching the fly with the hatch is one of the most important aspects of fly fishing. Equally important, however, is how that fly is presented to the trout. If the fish notices an unusual movement on the fly or sees the bright yellow fly line in the water, it will surely not bite.

Use a 10- to 12-foot-long (3- to 4-m-long) floating leader with a fine tippet that allows the fly to drift naturally. (When fishing with wet flies or streamers you won't need quite as long a leader [6 to 10 feet or 2 to 3 m], and the leader should sink.) Casting is all-important to the success of a dry-fly angler. The cast must be accurate and gentle so that the fly lands on the water without creating an unnatural disturbance. As the fly drifts slowly with the current, keep the line taut enough so that you can react in case of a strike, but not so tight as to create drag and alter the drift.

Brown Trout

This brown breaks the surface after being hooked with a spoon. While browns are the favorite among fly anglers, many people still fish for them using lures and natural baits.

Dry-fly fishing is perhaps the most difficult type of fishing to master, and the brown trout is the dry-fly angler's most adept opponent. The skills of casting, presentation, and fly selection take years of practice and experience to master, yet the sense of accomplishment one feels when hooking a big brownie with a dry fly makes it all worthwhile.

While the brown trout is the chief quarry of the fly enthusiast, many anglers do go after them using natural bait, spinning lures, and spoons. The best all-around natural bait, especially for large browns, is a dead or live minnow fished on medium-weight spinning or bait-casting tackle. Other good natural baits include nightcrawlers, crawfish, frogs, and various insects. The less terminal tackle you use, the better your chances will be. Don't use snaps or swivels, and if at all possible use only small split-shot sinkers.

In order to produce a strike you must get the bait as close to the fish's nose as possible while creating a minimum of disturbance. To do this, cast your bait upstream from the area you are about to fish. As the line drifts downstream, raise and lower the rod tip to put a little action on the bait and to keep it from snagging. Once the bait settles in the deep water of the hole, hold it there for ten to fifteen minutes before retrieving, using short, jerky movements.

When fishing with artificial lures, use the same method as described above for natural bait. Various types of small spinners, spoons, jigs, underwater plugs, and plastic lures may work well. These can be especially effective for going after large browns in the fall.

Since its introduction in North America, the brown trout has quickly become the most abundant fish on the continent. It can be found in hundreds of thousands of streams, rivers, and lakes in virtually every state of the United States and throughout most of Canada. The Great Lakes and their surrounding tributary streams and rivers offer some of the best brownie fishing in the world. Every year these waters are extensively stocked with browns who go on to establish natural populations. One of the most famous of all brown trout streams in eastern North America is the Beaverkill in upstate New York. This Catskill Mountain stream is visited by thousands of serious, novice, and intermediate fly anglers every year. Many anglers consider the Beaverkill nothing short of an historical monument, where serious fly fishing for browns began. Gordon, Hewitt, LaBranche, Hendrickson, Cross, Steenrod, Dettes, Darbees—these are just a few of the most famous names in angling history that are inextricably linked to the Beaverkill.

There has been a recent controversy, however, surrounding a planned housing development along the banks of the Beaverkill in Rockland and Col-

Trout

The Beaverkill in New York State is perhaps the most famous brown trout stream in North America. Recently, however, the stream's trout populations are being threatened by planned housing developments.

chester Townships. A New Jersey developer has bought about 2,100 acres (8,500 ha) on or near the Beaverkill with the intention of building a housing development. Conservationists and anglers alike believe that such development on a river as old and sensitive as the Beaverkill will raise water temperatures enough to effectively wipe out the brown trout population. The first phase of the battle is being waged in the Town of Rockland Planning Board, where the developer is hoping to change zoning restrictions so that he can build an initial thirty houses. While these thirty homes alone may not pose an immediate threat to the brown trout, they will enable the developer to expand his development into neighboring Colchester Township, where zoning laws are virtually nonexistent.

It is true that the brown trout is a sturdy fish, able to withstand higher levels of pollution and warmer temperatures than other types of trout, yet its future may be in jeopardy if current development threats, such as the one on the Beaverkill, are not soon curtailed or even reversed.

Chapter 6

Cutthroat

The cutthroat is not a particularly large fish. It doesn't put up nearly as spectacular a fight as does its distant cousins the rainbow and the steelhead, nor is it a particularly selective feeder or difficult to catch, like the brown trout. Like the brook trout, its numbers are quickly dwindling. Yet, there is a certain mystique surrounding this colorful fish, and it remains a prized catch among West Coast anglers.

Perhaps part of this mystique has to do with the fact that the cutthroat is considered the one true native Rocky Mountain fish. In fact, the cutthroat is commonly known to most western anglers simply as "the native." In addition, the angler must often hike through miles of scenic, mountainous terrain in order to find what are reportedly good cutthroat waters. And once found, there is no guarantee that most of the "natives" have not already been forced out by the more aggressive rainbows and browns. Yet whether or not a cutthroat expedition is successful or not, there is always a sense of adventure in going after this sometimes elusive fish. When fishing for cutthroats, the old adage almost always applies: "Getting there is half the fun."

This native North American fish can be found in coastal areas from southern Alaska to northern California and in inland lakes, rivers, and streams from southern British Columbia and Alberta south to New

CUTTHROAT

Left: *A true native of the Rocky Mountain region, cutters can be caught on the Yellowstone River.*
Below: *The cutthroat gets its name from a bright red or red-orange slash of color on its lower jaw, just under the dentary bone.*

Mexico. Cutthroats are found naturally from central Colorado west to mountainous regions of eastern California, although the fish has been introduced in the more western parts of California, as well. The best areas for fishing for sea-run cutthroats are the Campbell and Nimpkish rivers in British Columbia. Snake River, Wyoming, the Indian Peaks Wilderness Area in Wyoming and Utah, and Yellowstone Lake and other surrounding lakes are best for inland natives.

The cutthroat, or *Salmo clarki*, gets its name from the bright red or red-orange slash of color on its lower jaw, just under the dentary bone. This mark is particularly visible in males during the spawning season. Its elongate, terete body has a dark olive back and silvery olive sides. During the spawning season, the male's sides may contain a reddish to yellow-orange tint. The cutthroat also has several small, dark spots on its back, sides, and median fins.

While some cutthroats do migrate to marine and estuarine waters, the majority of them can be found in alpine lakes, rivers, and streams. Even the cutthroats that do make it to saltwater areas are not truly migratory fish in the same sense as steelhead or salmon. They do not make predictable yearly runs between salt water and spawning grounds. Instead, their travels are determined by the availability of food. They gradually swim downstream in search of food until their journey leads them out to sea. And once at sea, they very seldom travel more than a few miles from the mouth of their native stream or river. This same search for food may also bring them back into fresh water. Many times they return in the spring for the salmon fry hatch, when the salmon are spawning, or in the summer, during certain insect hatches. One thing is certain every year—they will always return to fresh water to spawn during the months of February and March.

Trout

The building of dams and dikes has blocked access to cutthroat spawning waters. Today, the angler must travel to relatively remote areas to find natural populations of cutthroat trout.

Unlike their coastal counterparts, inland cutthroats spawn in April and May. Both varieties reach four years of age before spawning, and then spawn on alternate years. The average life span of the cutthroat is approximately eight to ten years. Young cutthroat feed on a wide variety of insect larvae and tiny freshwater shrimp. When they grow older, they feed almost exclusively on other fish and fish eggs, only going for insects during large hatches.

The largest cutthroat ever caught with a rod and reel was a 30-inch-long (80-cm-long), 41-pounder (15-kg) pulled from Pyramid Lake, Nevada, in 1925. That particular strain of cutthroat, however, is now extinct. Today, it is rare that anyone catches a cutt larger than 5 pounds (2 kg). Most varieties grow no longer than 15 inches (40 cm) and weigh only 1 or 2 pounds (up to three-quarters of a kilogram). Catching a 5-pounder (2-kg) is considered quite an achievement.

As stated earlier, the numbers of this once-prolific fish are rapidly dwindling. While the cutthroat fits

This nicely sized cutthroat was caught with a fly outfit on Henry's Lake in Idaho.

into its own environment very well, it is not a very adaptable fish. Small changes in its native waters or the introduction of foreign species can mean doom for the cutthroat. The building of dams and dikes has blocked access to spawning grounds and destroyed or altered sensitive feeding areas. And, as with the brook trout, pollution has also taken a major toll. The cutthroat requires very clean, pristine waters in order to survive. The encroachment of civilization on prime fisheries and the long-distance pollution problems of acid rain and ozone depletion are altering the temperature and purity of streams and rivers across the continent. The first victims of these increasing problems are highly susceptible fish species such as the cutthroat and the brook trout.

The fact that the cutthroat is very sensitive to its environment also means that it is not easily transplanted. Most attempts at raising cutthroats in hatcheries and then transplanting them into the wild have failed miserably. The majority of hatcheries now devote their resources to raising browns and rainbows for use in stocking programs. While such programs have ensured a steady flow of trout for the angler, they have also helped contribute to the demise of cutthroat. Cutthroat hybridize very easily with other trout, especially the rainbow, which is a distant cousin. As cutthroats increasingly spawn with rainbows, the gene pool eventually becomes diluted and very few pure natives remain.

In addition, cutthroat waters are quickly being taken over by aggressive and prolific brown trout. These European transplants are very territorial fish that will stake a claim to a section of stream and chase out any intruding natives (see Chapter 5). The more timid and vulnerable cutthroat simply cannot compete with browns in prime feeding waters. Browns, rainbows, and steelhead all feed voraciously on the small cutthroat fry.

Anglers themselves also pose a threat to the cutthroat. The native can withstand heavy fishing pressure even less than other trout. It is a very good eating fish, so for many years anglers were more apt to keep their cutthroat catch than other, less tasty trouts such as the brown. Over the years, fish and game commissions have tried to remedy this situation by placing strict size and bag limits on the cutthroat while encouraging anglers to keep other competitive fish. One river commission in the Rocky Mountains even coined the phrase, "Kill a brown and save the cutthroat." And in one beaver pond in the Rocky Mountain National Park, they went as far as to intentionally poison other species of trout in an attempt to restore cutthroat populations. While this drastic measure

TROUT

> "Were it not that it [the cutthroat] occurs in the same area as two of the hardest fighting game fish known, its qualities would be more highly regarded. At times it does leap from the water when hooked, and often puts up quite a prolonged struggle before being landed. It generally rises quite readily to the fly, although as a rule it takes the fly sunk and drawn as a minnow more readily than the dry fly."
>
> J.R. Dymond,
> *Game Fish of British Columbia*

As with the brook trout, the existence of the cutthroat has been threatened by pollution and the encroachment of civilization.

worked temporarily, the other species of trout soon returned and again drove out the cutthroat.

Another threat comes from anglers who use live minnows that are not native to a particular stream or lake. When foreign minnows escape, they can quickly form large colonies that feed on cutthroat eggs, thus tipping nature's delicate balance.

Despite all of these threats to their existence, cutthroat populations remain large enough so that fishing for them is not yet illegal (or immoral). The cutthroat angler should, however, be conservation minded when catching this imperiled fish. Always release what you catch. While natives are great in the frying pan, they are even better alive in the water. Use barbless hooks and take care when removing the hook from the fish's mouth. Hold the fish gently in the water until it regains its senses and then release it. Never fish for natives during their spawning season. If you do hook a roe-laden female, take extra care when returning her to the water.

Like rainbow trout, natives enjoy strong, fast currents when living in

Trout

Cutthroats like to hold around obstructions such as large boulders and submerged logs as well as at the heads and tails of white water sections. This cutthroat (below) was caught with a rubber spider.

streams and rivers. They can often be found holding at the heads and tails of white-water sections. They also hold behind rocks and logs that split the strong currents. An extremely skittish fish, natives rarely venture too far from obstructions and cover. In addition, cutthroats tend to stay away from deep pools where a large, hostile brown may have staked its claim. They will, however, sit around the edges of a pool, looking for stray minnows that may come their way.

While they occasionally feed on the surface during large insect hatches, natives are primarily underwater feeders. Wet flies and nymphs fished just below the surface are a good bet for spring fishing. Because cutthroats are not particularly selective eaters, your choice of fly pattern is not quite so important as it is with other trout. However, it is always good to have a variety of flies on hand, just in case your old standbys aren't working on a particular day. Some good wet flies for the cutthroat include Woolly Worm, March Brown, Ginger Quill, Quill Gordon, Grizzly King, and Hendrickson. Good nymph patterns include Brown Stonefly, Ted's Stonefly, Caddis Larvae, and Gray Nymph.

During the late summer and early fall, the larger cutthroats feed almost entirely on minnows, freshwater shrimp, and other small fish. This is when small streamers and bucktails seem to work the best. In fact, streamers are fairly dependable flies at any time of year, when nothing else seems to work. Again, here, the type of streamer doesn't really matter all that much; however, you may want to use streamers that are slightly smaller than those you would use for steelhead or browns.

When fishing for cutthroats, the choice of fly is not nearly as important as its presentation. The native is perhaps the most easily frightened of all trout (and trout are a pretty frightened lot!). Any type of unnatural sound or movement will send it swimming for cover. Even the thin shadow of a fly line cast across the stream could ruin the fishing for an entire afternoon. Because of this, you should always use a long leader, at least 11 or 12 feet (3 m), and cast very delicately and accurately.

One method of streamer fishing, which avoids the cast altogether, can be very effective against the native. Stand upstream a good 40 to 50 feet (12 to 15 m) from the section you are about to fish. Use at least an 11-foot (3-m) leader and a small streamer, say a Muddler Minnow. Then simply drop the fly into the water and begin stripping out line, letting the streamer drift downstream into the fishing hole. As it reaches the hole, put a short, jerky action on it so that it darts forward and back, like a small minnow fighting to swim upstream. Fish with it like this for several minutes before slowly pulling it in, using the short, jerky action. Always be patient, and fish a hole for several casts, especially if you know the fish are there. It may take the first few casts just to get the native interested, and then a few more casts before the

The cutthroat is not a picky eater, but it is easily frightened; therefore, the choice of the fly is not nearly as important as its presentation. Any unusual sound or movement will send the cutthroat swimming for cover.

wary fish gets up enough nerve to attempt a strike.

Today, the majority of the inland cutthroats reside in alpine lakes, such as Yellowstone Lake or the small lakes of the Indian Peaks Wilderness area. They normally stay in shallow-water sections when feeding, and then move into deeper water during the summer months. Even in the midst of a hot summer, however, cutthroat do not move into the deepest sections of the lake, instead they hold around the edges of deep drop-offs or in deep sections of a shoal or reef.

The best time of year to catch lake-bound cutthroat is during the spring or fall, when they are actively patrolling the shoreline and shallow water for food. Cutthroat will always be moving when searching for food, because lakes do not have currents to deliver the food to them. Through observation it is sometimes possible to figure the feeding circuit a particular group of cutts may be making. Once this is accomplished, it is relatively easy to cast your fly to the spot where the fish is about to swim.

Trout

© Erwin & Peggy Bauer

CUTTHROAT

The best cutthroat waters are usually cold, clear mountain streams, far from civilization. Here a couple of anglers camp near a stream in Wyoming.

The *best* cutthroat fishing usually takes place on cloudy, cool, drizzly days. These fish are slightly light sensitive and will not feed as readily under a bright, warm sun. When searching the shorelines of a lake, keep an eye out for schools of minnows, large gatherings of water insects, or weed beds full of freshwater shrimp. Chances are there will be cutthroats lurking nearby, ready to feast on the quarry.

Even if the fish are feeding on the top, it is best to use nothing but wet flies in lakes. If you notice the fish nipping the surface of the lake, then fish your wet fly just below the surface film. If they are feeding deep, then work your fly along the bottom.

Some of the most exciting cutthroat fishing can be had in the Northwestern rivers that open to the sea. These rivers contain sea-run cutthroats, which tend to be larger, stronger, and more determined fighters than their solely freshwater counterparts. While not as exciting a fish as the steelhead, sea-run cutthroats have been known to strike hard and fast and occasionally jump. Sea-run natives are short, thick fish that average 2 pounds (1 kg) or more. They have a silver-white belly and a heavily spotted olive brown back. The best two rivers for sea-run cutthroat are the Nimpkish and the Campbell rivers, both in British Columbia.

While the future of the cutthroat is somewhat tentative, they still remain a good fall-back fish for the ardent angler. In the right waters, they can usually be found in virtually any type of weather, during any season of the year. And if you can find them, you can most certainly catch them. All anglers should, however, practice extreme care when fishing natives. Fish for them using fly tackle only (it gives the fish a better chance and creates more of an angling challenge for the angler) and always put back what you catch. If you do use bait, be careful not to use minnows or other live baits that may be foreign to the local environment. One or two simple observances by a number of concerned anglers can make a difference in helping to save this dwindling Rocky Mountain native.

Chapter 7

The lake trout

Few anglers have had the opportunity to visit any of the wilderness lakes in Canada's Northwest Territories. Just a few miles from the arctic circle, many of these lakes are free of ice for only two or three months a year,

While the best lake trout fishing takes place in the far northern regions of North America, such as Nakell Lake in Katmai, Alaska (left), good-sized lakers can be taken from lakes as far south as the Finger Lakes in New York (right).

and can only be reached by airplane or helicopter. Even in the height of the warm season, the water is frigid and the waves are choppy, and any form of modern civilization is at least hundreds, maybe thousands, of miles away. Yet, any angler who is resourceful enough and lucky enough to get there will be in for a fishing experience without equal. For lakes such as Great Bear and Athabasca are the homes of the colossal, fork-tailed Lake Trout, the largest char in North America.

Like the brook trout, the lake trout is not a member of the trout family at all. Its scientific name, *Salvelinus namaycush* places it in the char group. The lake trout's other common names include Mackinaw, togue, namaycush, Great Lakes trout, gray trout, salmon trout, forktail trout, and laker.

True to its name, the lake trout is a pelagic, or open-water fish that resides in lakes and other large bodies of water and seldom ventures into rivers or streams. Its back and sides are dark olive to gray and its belly is usually blue-gray to greenish bronze. On top of its dark coloring, the lake trout is covered with cream-colored spots on its head, body, adipose fin, and median fins. Some of the larger and older lake trout lose most of their markings and can be almost completely black. The edges of the laker's pectoral, pelvic, and anal fins are usually reddish orange with narrow white edges.

Perhaps the most distinguishing characteristics of the lake trout are its immense size and fork-shaped tail. It is one of the largest of all North American freshwater fishes. Commercial fishermen in northern Canada have netted lakers as heavy as 120 pounds (45 kg) and as long as 5 feet (2 m), and lakers from 30 to 40 pounds (11 to 15 kg) are quite commonplace. The rod and reel record for this hefty fish is 65 pounds (24 kg), a monster caught by Karry Daunis in Great Bear Lake, Canada.

Because the laker thrives in very deep, cold lakes with clean, highly oxygenated water, its range is somewhat limited. Most large laker populations are found in the lakes of Alaska, Canada, the Great Lakes, and Maine. The fish has also been introduced into other states as far south as Connecticut and New York, and as far west as the Rockies. This deep-water fish, however, cannot survive in water that gets any hotter than 60°F (15°C), so any attempts to introduce the fish into more southerly regions have been fruitless.

At one time there was a huge population of lakers in the Great Lakes; however, pollution and the proliferation of the lamprey eel have taken their toll. The lamprey, whose numbers greatly expanded in the Great Lakes during the 1940s, attaches itself to sides of the lake trout and sucks out its blood. The once-massive populations of these vam-

The Lake Trout

piric predators have recently been brought under control. This, in addition to stricter pollution standards, are helping to bring the lake trout back into the Great Lakes.

An even more unusual threat to the laker exists in the cold lakes of northern Canada. Here, one of this cannibalistic fish's main food supplies is its own offspring. A problem arises, however, when too many of the older, breeding-age fish are killed by anglers or by pollution. When this happens, not enough young fish can be produced to feed the entire population and the lake trout literally starves itself out. In addition, the older fish that do survive eat a disproportionate number of the already depleted younger fish, destroying the future of its own species. Because of the delicate nature of this type of food chain, Cana-

The Lake Trout

The lake trout can be most easily distinguished by its immense size and forked tail. Note the lamprey scar on the midsection of this lake trout. In remote northern lakes, commercial fishermen have netted lakers as large as 120 pounds (45 kg).

dian fishing authorities have put strict regulations on the number of lakers an angler can take.

The lake trout spawns in the fall, sometimes at depths of up to 100 feet (30 m). Unlike other types of char and salmon, the laker does not build a redd (egg depository). Instead, the female sweeps clean a small section of the gravelly bottom with gentle strokes of her tail. She then lays hundreds of tiny eggs, which are only a few millimeters in diameter. The eggs take anywhere from forty to 160 days to incubate, depending on the water temperature. The colder the temperature, the longer the incubation period. During this time, many of the eggs are destroyed by suckers, small lakers, or other fish. Even after they are hatched, the small fry may fall victim to other fish and even their own elders. In addition, these young fish are extremely sensitive to light and stay in deep waters for several months, until their eyes are fully developed.

The lake trout is perhaps the least popular and most unfamiliar of all trout for the average angler. The fish's

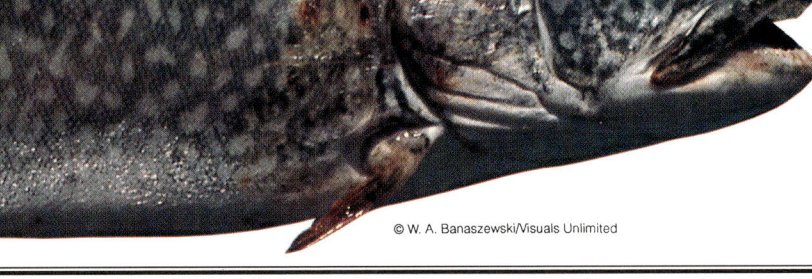

Trout

In recent years, ambitious stocking programs have greatly increased the numbers of lake trout in the Great Lakes region of the United States and Canada. Here a Minnesota Fish and Wildlife official releases some young lakers.

limited range makes it extremely difficult for many anglers to find suitable laker waters. The best lakes for these fish are in the remote wilderness areas of northern Canada, some of which are only accessible by helicopter or dog sled. It is in these lakes where most of the 40- to 60-pounders (15- to 22-kg) can be found. There are, however, many other, more readily accessible lakes throughout Canada and the northern United States, where good-sized lakers (20 to 40 pounds [8 to 15 kg]) are readily caught. For the freshwater angler who wants to catch really big fish and is willing to do some traveling, there is simply nothing like the lake trout.

The best lake trout fishing usually takes place in the early spring or fall, when the water is still cold and the fish can be found in the shallower sections of the lake. In the fall, however, the fishing is not usually good until after the spawning season. During the actual spawning time, the fish are too concerned with reproducing to feed very much.

In the United States, the best months for lake trout are April and

The Lake Trout

Greater pollution controls and the reduction of lamprey eel populations have brought lake trout fishing back to the Great Lakes. Here (right) an angler fishes for lakers and salmon on the north shore of Lake Superior.

May, and then again in October and November. During the warm summer months the fish move into colder waters between 100 and 200 feet (30 to 60 m) deep and can only be taken by trolling or jigging. In Canada and Alaska, however, where the water stays cold year round, good fishing can be had throughout the summer.

The lake trout is known as a foul-weather fish. The worse the weather, the easier they are to catch. Many anglers will only fish for these big lunkers on cold, rainy, windy days, especially if the fish are holding in shallow waters.

Fishing for lake trout does not require a great deal of skill on the part of the angler. In fact, the most difficult aspect of this type of fishing is simply locating the fish. If you are new to a particular lake, it is best to hire an experienced fishing guide or, at the very least, talk to local fishermen, tackle store owners, or the local fish and game commission. Lake trout usually follow a regular pattern in their home lake. Once you know their routes you should have few problems locating and catching them.

Trout

The Lake Trout

Lake trout love to hold craggy bottoms strewn with sharp rocks and boulders. Also look for them near reefs and shoals that drop off into deep water.

In the early spring, lake trout can usually be found feeding near the shore or along reefs and shoals at the edges of steep drop-offs. They will almost never hold along shorelines or reefs that are not in direct contact with deep water. In addition, lakers prefer craggy bottoms strewn with large boulders and sharp rocks. The more jagged the reef or shoal, the better the fishing will be.

For fishing reefs and shoals, you will need a 5- to 6-foot (2-m), medium-weight bait-casting rod loaded with about 200 feet (60 m) of 18-pound (8-kg) test line. Lake trout are not picky eaters, so virtually any type of large spoon (from 4 to 6 inches [15 cm]) will do. Yellow, red, orange, and pink lures can be particularly effective on overcast days. Natural baits such as suckers, smelt, yellow perch, chubs, alewives, darters, and shiners also work well when fishing the shallow areas.

The best fishing areas are underwater reefs that are surrounded by deep water on all sides. When exploring these areas from a boat, look for dark areas of water within the shallow areas. These are deep water holes, which usually contain several large fish. As a general rule, however, the larger trout hold on the outer edges of the shoal or reef while the smaller fish are scattered throughout. Even if you have your heart set on catching a 20- to 30-pounder (8- to 11-kg) it is best to fish the shallow areas first before going after the larger fish in deep water.

Begin by situating your boat in the deep water outside the shoal and cast in toward the shallow water. There is debate as to whether a slow or a fast retrieve is best. Some anglers believe that a slow retrieve will attract more fish, but may not get as many hits because the fish has time to examine the lure. When going for the faster retrieve the fish will tend to hit harder and faster, but the bait may not get as many looks. The best advice is to experiment and see what works best in a particular hole on a particular day.

Once you have adequately covered the shallow water, move your boat to the inside of the shoal or reef and fish out to the deeper waters. The rule is

Trout

Always carry several different spoons in your tackle box. Because you need to fish your lures very close to the bottom, chances are you will snag and lose several lures during each outing. A depth finder, such as the one on this boat (opposite page), will make the job of locating lake trout much easier.

to fish from the outside in (cast from the deep water into the shallow water) and then change position and fish from the inside out (cast from the shallow water into the deep water), the logic being that if you move the boat directly into the shallow water you will scare away more fish.

Because lake trout only eat on or near the bottom, always fish as deep as you can without regularly getting snagged. Chances are you will get snagged quite often (and leave your share of spoons on the bottom) no matter how carefully you fish. In fact, if you never get snagged, you are probably not fishing deep enough.

As the summer sets in and the water warms up, lake trout abandon the shallow reefs and shoals for the dark, cool deep waters. They stay almost exclusively in the thermocline layer of the lake, where the water is rich in oxygen and stays at about 50°F (10°C). These hefty fish may be holding anywhere from 50 to 200 feet (15 to 60 m) deep, depending on the climate and the water temperature. At this time of year, trolling is by far the most effective method for going after lakers. For deep-water trolling you will need a 6½- to 7-foot (2-m) trolling or heavy bait rod loaded with 300 to 400 feet (90 to 120 m) of 15- to 20-pound (7- to 9-kg) test wire or lead core line. The deeper the water you are trolling, the heavier pound test line you will need.

The most effective lures for deep-water trolling are large 4- to 6-inch (10- to 15-cm) spoons. You can use natural baits such as suckers, alewives, smelt, chubs, and yellow perch. It is also good to add one or more attractor spinners, or "cowbells," to your rig to gain even more attention.

As with casting for lakers, the most difficult part of trolling is locating the fish. As stated before, they almost always stay in the thermocline layer in the summer. The depth of this layer can vary from lake to lake, or even in different sections of the same lake, depending on water

The Lake Trout

currents and weather. Two near-essential pieces of equipment are a depth finder and a temperature probe. By scanning the lake with these two devices, you can usually determine about where the fish are. If an underwater ridge or reef falls at the thermocline, you should fish that section for quite a while. Chances are, it is strewn with lake trout. Also, keep an eye out for signs of alewife schools. Where there is plenty of food, there are usually lakers.

The process of trolling is really quite simple. You just lower your lure to the desired depth (the thermocline), and then move the boat across or against the current at a slow speed. As you troll, put a little action on the lure by raising and lowering your rod tip at regular intervals.

If you don't have the aid of a depth finder and temperature probe, then finding the lakers is more or less a

Trout

The Lake Trout

Jigging from a small boat (opposite page) is an extremely popular method for catching lake trout. Here a pair of anglers jig for lakers off the Kenai Peninsula, Alaska. Right: A wildlife official displays a 6-pound (2-kg) stocker just before releasing him into the wild. Below: Mr. J., by Luhr Jensen.

process of trial and error. First, lower your lure until it hits bottom, then reel it in a few feet. Troll at that depth for a while. If you don't get any hits, raise the lure a few more feet. Keep experimenting at different depths until you find the fish. Once the proper depth is located, mark it on your line with a piece of tape so that you can fish it consistently.

Jigging is another popular method for taking deep-water lakers. As with trolling, the actual fishing procedure for jigging is very simple. Drift your boat above a deep reef, shoal, or any jagged drop-off where you think the fish are feeding. Lower your lure over the edge and into the deep water until it hits bottom, then begin working it up and down with your rod tip and reel. Slowly reel it in and lower it down, eventually bringing it up through the thermocline and back down again. Don't hurry your jig. Lake trout have been known to see a jig hit bottom and then follow it up through the thermocline and almost to the surface before striking. The longer your lure is in the water, the better your chances of catching a fish.

Part of the attraction of jigging is that you can use lighter equipment than with trolling (meaning a slightly more dramatic fight from the trout), and jigging doesn't require the use of a motorboat. It can be done quite effectively from a rowboat. The best jigging outfit is a 5- to 6-foot (2-m) medium-weight bait-casting or spinning rod, loaded with about 200 feet (60 m) of 18-pound (8-kg) test line (the amount and poundage of your line depends on how deep you are fishing; however, the setup mentioned here should be good for most situations). Again here, a large 4-inch (10-cm) spoon or a light-colored, heavy-sinking lure will work well. Add a spinner or two, and/or a piece of sucker, and you will have a very tempting jigging rig.

While the lake trout seems to be on the rebound in the United States—especially in the Great Lakes and in New York's Finger Lakes—Canada is still the place to go for really big lakers. Unfortunately, many of the very best laker waters (where a lucky troller can pull in a 40-pounder [18-kg]) are not easily accessible to the average angler. Even so, there are plenty of other, more approachable lakes in both the United States and Canada where 20- to 30-pounders (8- to 11-kg) are fairly common. As with most trout, however, the farther north you go, the bigger fish you find.

The lake trout does not require a great deal of skill or cunning to catch, and it won't always put up a huge fight (especially if you are using heavy-duty trolling equipment); however, few fishing experiences are equal to reeling in a trout so big that could quite easily feed a family of four.

Noted Lake Trout Waters

Province or State	Lake
Alberta	Cold Lake, Gris Lake, Peerless Lake, Swan Lake, and Wentzel Lake
Manitoba	Clearwater Lake, God's Lake, Nueltin Lake, Lake Athapapuskow, and Reed Lake
Northwest Territories	Great Bear Lake and Great Slave Lake
Quebec	Chibougamau Lake, Lake Mistassini, Lake St. John, and Lake Wakonichi
Saskatchewan	Black Lake, Cree Lake, Kingsmere Lake, Lac La Ronge, Lake Athabasca, Little Bear Lake, Reindeer Lake, and Waterbury Lake
Maine	Beech Hill Pond, Branch Lake, East Grand Lake, Moosehead Lake, Schoodic Lake, Sebec Lake, and West Grand Lake
Michigan	Crystal Lake, Elk Lake, Higgins Lake, and Torch Lake
New Hampshire	Big Greenbough Pond, Newfound Lake, Silver Lake, Squam Lake, and Tarlton Lake
New York	Canandiagua Lake, Cayuga Lake, Keuka Lake, Lake George, Raquette Lake, and Seneca Lake
Wisconsin	Green Lake

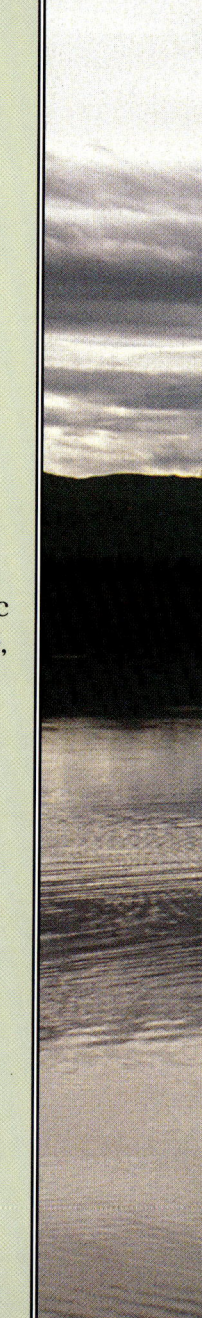

The Lake Trout

BIBLIOGRAPHY AND RECOMMENDED READING

Bergman, Ray, *Trout*. New York: Knopf, 1976.

Evanoff, Vlad, *The Freshwater Fisherman's Bible*. New York: Doubleday, 1980.

Flick, Art, *Art Flick's Streamside Guide to Naturals and Their Imitations*. New York: Crown Publishers, 1970.

Gierach, John, *Trout Bum*. New York: Fireside Books/Simon & Schuster, 1988.

Ginrich, Arnold, *The Well-Tempered Angler*. New York: Plume, 1987.

Hackle, Sparse Grey, *Fishless Days, Angling Nights*. New York: Fireside Books/Simon & Schuster, 1988.

Haig-Brown, Roderick L., *A River Never Sleeps*. New York: Crown Publishers, 1974.

Kaufmann, Randall, *Fly Tyers Nymph Manual*. Western Fisherman's Press, 1986.

LaFontaine, Gary, *Caddisflies*. New York: Winchester, 1981.

Leiser, Eric, *The Complete Book of Fly Patterns*. New York: Knopf, 1977.

Lilly, Bud and Paul Schullery, *Bud Lilly's Guide to Western Fly-Fishing*. New York: Lyons & Burford, 1987.

Lyons, Nick, *Bright Rivers*. New York: Fireside Books/Simon & Schuster, 1977.

Lyons, Nick, *The Seasonable Angler*. New York: Fireside Books/Simon & Schuster, 1988.

Bibliography and Recommended Reading

Maclean, Norman, *A River Runs Through It*. Chicago: University of Chicago Press, 1983.

Marinaro, Vince, *In the Ring of the Rise*. New York: Crown Publishers, 1976.

Ovington, Ray, *Tactics on Trout*. New York: Scribners, 1969.

Raymond, Steve, *The Year of the Trout*. New York: Fireside Books/Simon & Schuster, 1988.

Rosenthal, Mike, *North America's Freshwater Fishing Book*. New York: Scribner, 1984.

Schaffner, Herbert, *The Fishing Tackle Catalog: A Sourcebook for the Well-Equipped Angler*. New York: Gallery Books, 1989.

Schullery, Paul, *American Fly Fishing: A History*. New York: Nick Lyons Books, 1987.

Schwiebert, Ernest G., *Nymphs*. Winchester Press, 1973 (out of print).

Soucie, Gary, *Soucie's Fishing Databook: Essential Facts for Better Fresh & Saltwater Fishing*. New York: Winchester Press, 1985.

Swisher, Doug and Carl Richards, *Selective Trout*. New York: Crown, 1971.

Traver, Robert, *Trout Madness*. New York, Fireside Books/Simon & Schuster, 1960.

Traver, Robert, *Trout Magic*. New York: Fireside Books/Simon & Schuster, 1974.

INDEX

A

American Fishing Tackle Manufacturers Association, 19

B

Bait
  for brook trout, 39
  for brown trout, 91
  for rainbow trout, 53, 58–59
  for steelhead, 73–75
Bait-casting tackle, 27–29
Bamboo fly rods, 17
Beaverkill (river), development along, 91–93
Bergman, Ray, 11
Boats, 59, 117–21
Brook trout, 31–45
  color and markings, 34
  ease of catching, 36
  feeding patterns, 39
  fly fishing for, 36–39
  habitat and range, 32, 40–43
  hatchery breeding, 33
  human encroachment on, 32–33
  in salt water, 35
  scientific classification, 34
  seasonal catching, 40
  size, 35
  skittishness of, 36
  spawning period, 45
  water temperature for, 43
Brown trout, 80–93
  bait for, 91
  catching difficulty, 84
  color and markings, 83
  cutthroat and, 99
  feeding, 85
  first appears in North America, 81–82
  fly fishing for, 85–87, 90–91
  habitat, 88
  human encroachment on, 91–93
  intelligence of, 85
  rainbow trout and, 83–84
  range, 83, 91
  scientific classification, 83
  spawning, 83
  stocking, 91
  in stocking programs, 84–85
  territoriality, 88
Bucktails
  for brook trout, 39
  for rainbow trout, 54

C

Caledonia hatchery, 82
Casting techniques
  for lake trout, 118–19
  for rainbow trout, 55–56
  for steelhead, 77
Cold Spring Harbor Hatchery, 82
Compleat Angler, The (Walton), 11, 85
Cutthroat, 94–107
  brown trout and, 99
  color and markings, 97
  conservation measures, 99–101
  dwindling numbers, 98–99
  failure in hatcheries, 99
  feeding habits, 103–4
  fishing techniques, 107
  fly fishing for, 104–7
  habitat, 101–3, 105
  human encroachment on, 98–99
  life span, 98
  migration by, 97
  range, 96–97
  size, 98
  spawning, 97–98

Index

D

Double-taper line, 19
Dry flies
   for brook trout, 39
   for rainbow trout, 53
Dymond, J.R., 100

E

Eastern brook trout. *See* Brook trout

F

Fiberglass rods, 17
Floating line, 20
Floating-sinking line, 20
Fly fishing, 14–16
   bait-casting tackle, 27–29
   for brook trout, 36–39
   for brown trout, 85–87, 90–91
   for cutthroat, 104–7
   flies, 22
   line density, 20
   line taper, 19
   line weight, 18–19
   for rainbow trout, 53
   reels, 20–21
   rods, 16–18
   spinning tackle, 24–27
   for steelhead, 76–78

G

Geirach, John, 11
Gilbert, William, 81–82
Graphite rods, 17

H

Hatcheries, 33, 82, 99

I

Intermediate line, 20

J

Jigging, for lake trout, 121

L

Lake trout, 108–23
   casting techniques, 118–19
   characteristics, 110
   fishing areas and techniques, 117–18
   jigging for, 121
   lamprey eels and, 110–12
   lures for, 118
   noted waters for, 122
   pollution and, 110
   range, 109-10
   scientific classification, 110
   seasonal fishing for, 114–15
   spawning, 113
   threats to, 112–13
   trolling, 119–21
   water temperature, 110
Lamprey eel, 110–12
Level line, 19
Line density, 20
Line taper, 19
Line weight, 18–19
Lures
   for lake trout, 118
   for steelhead, 73, 76

M

McCloud. *See* Rainbow trout
Maclean, Norman, 11
Mather, Fred, 82
Mountain trout. *See* Brook trout

N

Native trout. *See* Brook trout

P

Plunking, for rainbow trout, 58–59
Pollution, 33, 99, 110

R

Rainbow trout, 46–61
  bait for, 53
  as bottom feeders, 53
  brown trout and, 83–84
  casting techniques, 55–56
  color and markings, 48
  habitat and range, 48–50, 61
  plunking technique, 58–59
  scientific classification, 48
  seasonal catching, 54–55
  size, 49–50
  strains, 50
  water temperature, 57
Raymond, Steve, 11
Red trout. See Brook trout
Reels, 20–21
Richards, Carl, 22
River Runs Through It, A
    (MacLean), 11
Rods, 16–17
  length, 18
  line density, 20
  line taper, 19
  line weight, 18–19
  materials, 17

S

Salt water, brook trout in, 35
Selective Trout (Swisher and
    Richards), 22
Shooting taper line, 19
Sinking line, 20
Sink-tip line, 20
Speckled trout. See Brook trout
Spinning lures, for rainbow trout, 58
Spinning tackle, 24–27
Squaretails. See Brook trout
Steelhead, 62–79
  bait for, 73–75
  feeding and water levels, 71
  fly fishing for, 76–78
  jumping, 68–69
  lures for, 73
  popularity of, 67–68
  range, 67, 78
  "rest stops" for, 71–73
  spawning, 65–66
  as strain of rainbow trout, 66
  water temperature, 71
  winter run, 65, 66–67
Streamers
  for brook trout, 39
  for cutthroat, 104–5
  for rainbow trout, 54
Swisher, Doug, 22

T

Tackle
  baitcasting, 27–29
  spinning, 24–27
Trolling, for lake trout, 119–21
Trout
  habitat and range, 14
  nature of, 13–14
  See also specific types of trout
Trout (Bergman), 11
Trout Bum (Geirach), 11

V

Von Behr, F., 82

W

Walton, Isaac, 11, 85
Water levels, steelhead feeding and, 71
Weight forward line, 19
Wet flies, for rainbow trout, 54
Wet-fly patterns, for brook trout, 39

Y

Year of the Trout, The (Raymond), 11